ON MY HONOR

Transforming Leadership, Families, and Culture

BY MIKE DENKER

Dedicated to My Gorgeous Wife

Angel

Mi Vida Toda

ON MY HONOR

3

Contents

"Setting the Stage

In the bustling heart of a thriving metropolis, a once-proud organization stood at a crossroads, its legacy teetering on the edge of oblivion. This organization, a symbol of innovation and progress, was grappling with a dilemma that transcended profits and bottom lines. Its leadership team, once renowned for their acumen and dedication, now found themselves ensnared in a quagmire of discontent and distrust. A darkness hung over the corridors, a stark contrast to the vibrant energy that once defined this place.

The sun dipped below the horizon, casting long shadows across the office floors. It was clear that something fundamental had eroded within the company's culture. The spark that had fueled camaraderie and collaboration had dimmed, replaced by an undercurrent of skepticism and self-interest. The organization's once-loyal employees now glanced suspiciously over their shoulders, uncertainty clouding their eyes as they navigated the complexities of their roles.

The effects of this malaise were palpable. Employee morale plummeted, productivity waned, and innovation stagnated. The walls that once resonated with laughter and shared aspirations now seemed to echo with missed opportunities and unfulfilled potential. It was evident that a transformation was imperative— a renaissance that would rekindle the spirit of Honor and integrity that defined the organization's early days.

It was against this tumultuous backdrop that the notion of Honor was reintroduced, not as a lofty ideal, but as a practical and transformative force. This introduction of Honor, encapsulated in the five pillars of Habits, Offerings, Non-Negotiables, Others-Focus, and Reflection, became a guiding light—a map to navigate the treacherous waters and emerge on the shores of positive change.

We invite you to join us on a journey of discovery and redemption. This narrative isn't just about an organization—it's about leadership, families, and culture. It's about recognizing the catalysts that spark change, understanding the consequences of low Honor, and embracing the potential for renewal. We will explore how the essence of Honor can breathe life into even the most beleaguered of environments.

We will uncover the pivotal moments that set the wheels of transformation in motion, casting light on incidents and challenges that reveal the sobering truth: that low Honor is a corrosive force capable of unraveling the fabric of leadership and culture. This journey will compel you to reevaluate your own beliefs and actions, as we embark on a quest to unlock the potential of Honor.

Chapter 1: The Catalyst for Change

Amid the towering glass walls of the Danalgo headquarters, a sense of unease had taken root. Jake McLeash, the CEO, stood gazing out at the cityscape below. What was once a vibrant hub of innovation and teamwork now felt like a ship adrift in stormy seas. A growing dissonance among the leadership team had cast a dark cloud over the company's culture. "This ship is sinking. I'm going down with it."

The catalyst for transformation materialized one crisp morning during a high-stakes board meeting. As Jake took his seat at the head of the table, he noticed the strained expressions on the faces of his fellow executives. Samantha Knight, his trusted mentor and ardent supporter on the board, was uncharacteristically quiet. This was a stark departure from her usual spirited engagement.

The atmosphere grew strained as they worked through the agenda. As each item was discussed, Jake sensed an undercurrent of tension. Decisions that were once unanimous now sparked debates, and subtle hints of self-interest began to eclipse the company's overarching mission. Jake's instincts told him that something was amiss, something that transcended mere policy or strategy.

"Alright, let's discuss the launch strategy for the new product," Jake announced, trying to steer the conversation toward a constructive path.

Samantha leaned forward. "I have some serious concerns about this strategy. The market is changing rapidly, and I'm not convinced that our current approach is the right way to go."

Jake nodded. "Samantha, your insights are valuable. Could you share more about your concerns?"

Samantha continued. "We're investing significant resources into this launch, but what if the market shifts before we even get off the ground? We need to be more agile in our approach, ready to adapt to changes in real-time."

Mark, seated across the table, leaned back in his chair. "Samantha, I get where you're coming from, but we've done our research. The data supports our current strategy. We can't just keep changing direction every time the wind blows."

Samantha's voice carried an edge as she responded, "Mark, data is important, but it's not everything. We need to consider the intangibles—the changing consumer sentiment, the potential disruptions in the industry. Are we really willing to bet everything on this one approach?"

Mark's jaw tightened. "We're not betting everything. We're making a strategic move based on careful analysis. We can't afford to jump ship every time someone raises a concern."

As the back-and-forth continued, the room seemed to split into two camps—those aligned with Samantha's more cautious approach, and those who stood firmly by Mark's data-driven strategy. The discussion, which started as a conversation, escalated into a clash of perspectives.

What should have been a constructive discourse unraveled into a verbal showdown, each word a volley in a war of egos. The executives took sides, aligning themselves based not on the project's merits, but on personal allegiances.

The meeting ended in disarray, leaving Jake disheartened and deeply troubled. He knew that this incident was not isolated—it was emblematic of a broader malady that took root within the organization. The culture of Honor that had once united them had eroded, replaced by an environment of discord, distrust, and self-serving agendas.

As the days went on, the consequences of this low Honor culture became increasingly apparent. Employee morale plummeted, innovation stagnated, and teamwork dissolved into factionalism. The energy that had fueled Danalgo's rise was being sapped by internal strife, and Jake realized that the organization's very survival was at stake.

The realization hit him like a thunderbolt: for Danalgo to thrive once more, a radical transformation was imperative. The organization's culture needed a complete overhaul, and it began with the leadership. Jake knew that he couldn't effect this change alone; he needed a guide, someone who could navigate the treacherous terrain of rebuilding Honor from the ground up.

Jake reached out to Maddy Davidson, a woman of remarkable reputation and indomitable spirit. Maddy implemented the HONOR Code at organizations of all sizes and across diverse industries, and she achieved remarkable outcomes. The HONOR Code© was rooted in simplicity—the five pillars of Habits, Offerings, Non-Negotiables, Others-Focus, and Reflection. These pillars, when woven into the fabric of an organization, had the power to ignite a shift in culture. They arranged a meeting away from his office.

Jake stepped into the bustling coffee shop, his thoughts a whirlwind of uncertainties. As he glanced around, he noticed a woman sitting by the window, engrossed in a notebook. This was Maddy Davidson, the person he had heard so much about—a glimmer of hope in a sea of doubt.

He approached her table with a mix of anticipation and nervousness. "Maddy Davidson?"

Maddy looked up, her gaze warm and inviting. "You must be Jake. Please, have a seat."

As they settled across from each other, Jake started. "I've heard incredible things about you, Maddy. The way you've helped others rebuild their reputations... But my situation feels like uncharted territory. The company's Honor seems to have crumbled, and I don't even know where to begin."

Maddy leaned back, her expression empathetic. "Jake, I understand your concerns. Rebuilding Honor is a challenging journey, and it's not without resistance. People may doubt your intentions, and the path ahead will be filled with obstacles."

Jake sighed, his worry evident. "Is it even worth it? The company's legacy is tarnished, and the road to redemption seems steep and treacherous."

Maddy's eyes sparkled with determination. "Jake, the journey won't be easy, but it's always worth it. Rebuilding Honor is about more than just fixing a reputation; it's about restoring trust, fostering integrity, and setting a new standard for how things should be done. It's about demonstrating resilience in the face of challenges."

Jake's gaze met hers, searching for reassurance. "But what if we face resistance from within? What if the same people who contributed to the downfall are resistant to change?"

Maddy's voice was confident. "Resistance is a part of any transformational journey. But remember, change doesn't happen overnight. It takes patience, consistency, and a deep commitment to doing what's right. If you lead with integrity and a genuine desire to rebuild, you'll find that people will eventually come around."

Jake leaned forward, his doubt slowly giving way to curiosity. "And what role would you play in all of this?"

Maddy smiled, her energy infectious. "I'll be your guide, Jake. I've seen organizations rise from the ashes of their mistakes. I'll help you navigate the challenges, strategize the right moves, and inspire your team to embrace a new culture of Honor. It's about setting a course for a better future and showing that change is possible."

As the conversation continued, Jake found himself captivated by Maddy's resolute belief in the potential for transformation. Her words resonated with the teachings he had learned from his faith—to persevere in the face of adversity and to value the journey toward redemption.

As he left the coffee shop that day, Jake felt a newfound sense of purpose. The path ahead might be uncertain, but with Maddy by his side, he was determined to rebuild Honor from the ground up, drawing strength from his faith and the guidance of someone who had walked this path before.

With Maddy's guidance, Jake embarked on a journey that would challenge his preconceptions and demand his dogged commitment. Together, they would uncover the hidden consequences of low Honor in different leadership roles, navigating incidents that exposed the fault lines of the organization's foundation.

As the sun set on that fateful day, Jake McLeash stood a little taller. The catalyst for change had arrived, and he was ready to seize it. Armed with the guidance of Maddy Davidson and supported by Samantha Knight, he wanted to lead Danalgo on a transformative journey—one that would test the limits of leadership, integrity, and Honor itself.

The journey was about to begin.

Reflections 3-2-1

Lessons Learned: We embarked on a journey alongside Jake McLeash, the CEO of Danalgo, as he faced a company culture in disarray. We witnessed the catalyst for change that ignited the quest for transformation and explored the initial steps taken towards rebuilding a culture of Honor.

Key Takeaways:

1. **Recognition of Discontent:** The chapter highlights the critical importance of recognizing the signs of discord within an organization. Jake's unease and realization of a sinking ship underscore the need for leaders to be attentive to shifts in culture and dynamics.

2. **Leadership Accountability:** The exchange between Samantha and Mark demonstrates the need for leaders to navigate debates constructively, valuing input beyond data and embracing a diversity of viewpoints.

3. **Embrace of Transformation:** Jake's decision to seek the guidance of Maddy Davidson exhibits his commitment to restoring a culture of Honor. It is wise to seek external expertise to navigate the complexities of rebuilding a tarnished reputation.

Reflective Questions:

1. **Manage Conflict:** Consider a situation where you've witnessed disagreements within your leadership team. How effectively were those disagreements managed? Could alternative approaches have fostered more constructive discussions?

2. **Open to Help:** Put yourself in Jake's shoes: if faced with a similar predicament, would you be open to seeking external guidance, like Maddy Davidson? How might external expertise contribute to your efforts to transform organizational culture?

Compelling Action Steps:

1. **Foster Constructive Dialogue:** Embrace differences of opinion within your leadership team as opportunities for growth. Encourage open, respectful discussions that prioritize collective decision-making over individual agendas.

As we reflect, we see the significance of leadership's role in shaping organizational culture. The choices we make as leaders impact the immediate trajectory of our organizations and lay the foundation for a culture of Honor.

Chapter 2: The Journey Begins

Maddy Davidson stood before a diverse assembly of leaders, her gaze steady and fixed. The room buzzed a mixture of curiosity and skepticism. Before her stood an eclectic group—Vice Presidents, Division Leaders, Department Heads—all mainstays of Danalgo's leadership hierarchy. Each had their own narrative, their own experiences, and their own reservations about the path of high Honor that lay ahead.

The setting was the grand auditorium, a space that had seen countless presentations on strategy, innovation, and growth. But today was different. Today, Maddy was here to introduce a concept that transcended mere business objectives—it was about transforming the very essence of leadership, families, and culture.

With a calm and assured demeanor, Maddy began to speak. She described the framework of The HONOR Code©, its five pillars encapsulating a blueprint for a cultural renaissance. As she introduced each pillar, Habits, Offerings, Non-Negotiables, Others-Focus, and Reflection, her words resonated with a quiet power. She shared stories of organizations that had embraced this code, where leaders had shed their egos and embraced a higher purpose.

However, the initial response from the leaders was a mix of raised eyebrows, exchanged glances, and veiled skepticism. The notion of transforming their leadership approach based on values seemed too idealistic, too disconnected from the harsh realities of business and competition. The aura of skepticism clung to the room like a shadow, a silent voice asking whether this journey toward high Honor was even worth the effort.

As Maddy navigated through her presentation, she could sense the resistance in the room, the collective doubt that clouded the minds of these accomplished leaders. She knew that the transition from established routines to a new paradigm required more than mere words—it demanded a fundamental shift in mindset and perspective. Each leader carried their own baggage of past decisions and compromises, and breaking free from those chains would be no easy feat.

"Ladies and gentlemen, the crux of our challenge lies in navigating the divide that often separates our aspirations from our actions, and in reconciling the magnetic pull of a high Honor culture with the ease of sticking to what's familiar. I recognize that the journey of transformation I'm embarking upon with all of you needs to be anchored in pragmatic steps and tangible insights. It's not enough to merely talk about the allure of a culture of Honor; we need to live it, to breathe life into it through deliberate actions.

Let me share stories of leaders who stood precisely where you stand at Danalgo today. Like many of you, they greeted this concept with skepticism. They questioned whether a shift towards Honor was feasible amidst the complexities of our world. But as they embarked on the journey, they discovered that the transformation was not an abstract ideal, but a force that could enact change. Much like you, they were daunted by the uncertainties, the resistance from within, and the challenges that accompanied the path of change. However, they persevered, and their organizations flourished not just in reputation, but in their very essence.

So, let us remember that it's not enough to be enamored by the notion of Honor. We must be willing to translate it into our daily practices, to reshape our interactions and decisions, and to embrace the journey of change with staunch commitment. Together, we have the power to turn skepticism into belief, and belief into a legacy of Honor that will shape our organizations and our collective future."

Maddy's words were punctuated by anecdotes of leaders who faced similar struggles and doubts. The audience began to realize that they were not alone in their reservations, that the journey they were embarking upon was a shared one. As Maddy described the tumultuous process of self-assessment, reflection, and commitment to change, a quiet sense of introspection began to permeate the room.

The journey was not going to be easy. It would demand introspection, vulnerability, and a willingness to dismantle the barriers that shielded their egos. Each leader would need to confront their personal struggles and the ways in which they compromised their own values for short-term gains. Maddy's words planted the seeds of change, but the path ahead was fraught with challenges.

As the session came to an end, a palpable shift had occurred. The skepticism had not vanished, but it began to intertwine with curiosity and a glimmer of hope. The leaders dispersed, each carrying a weighty contemplation of the journey they were about to embark upon.

The journey toward high Honor had begun, and for Danalgo's leaders, the road ahead was uncertain, fraught with resistance, but undeniably filled with potential for transformation.

Reflections 3-2-1

Lessons Learned: In this chapter, we delved into the introduction of the concept of high Honor at Danalgo. We witnessed the initial skepticism and doubts among the leaders as they confronted the prospect of a transformative journey.

Key Takeaways:

1. **Transformation Amid Skepticism:** The chapter emphasized that introducing a new paradigm of leadership can be met with skepticism and resistance, especially when it challenges established routines.

2. **Shared Struggles:** We learned that leaders often share common doubts and reservations when faced with change, realizing that they are not alone in their apprehensions.

3. **Potential for Profound Change:** The chapter highlighted the potential for significant change through stories of leaders who have embraced transformation, despite their initial doubts.

Reflective Questions:

1. **Skepticism:** How do your own doubts and skepticism impact your willingness to embrace change in your leadership approach?

2. **Familiarity:** Have you ever felt torn between the allure of a new concept and the comfort of the familiar? How did you navigate this tension?

Compelling Action Step:

1. **Open Dialogue:** Initiate open dialogues with your colleagues and team members about their concerns and reservations regarding change, fostering an environment of shared vulnerability and understanding.

As we move forward on this journey of embracing high Honor, let us remember that change often begins amidst skepticism. The path ahead may be filled with challenges, but the stories of leaders who have turned skepticism into belief should inspire us to persevere. Our personal introspection and open dialogue will be vital in overcoming obstacles and embracing the transformative potential of this journey. Together, we have the power to shape a culture that values Honor, integrity, and growth.

Chapter 3: Business Leaders
From Self-Centered to Others-Focused

Within the hallowed halls of Danalgo, a transformation was underway—one that would redefine the very essence of leadership. The journey that Maddy Davidson embarked upon with the organization's leaders was an exploration of values, integrity, and the path from self-centeredness to embracing a higher purpose.

As the weeks progressed, the leaders found themselves facing a series of reflective exercises that probed the depths of their actions, motivations, and decisions. Encouraged by Maddy's guidance, they set aside their egos and explored the labyrinthine recesses of their own characters. Each leader confronted their own moments of compromise, their instances of prioritizing personal gain over the greater good.

Jake McLeash, as CEO, was no exception. He revisited decisions made in pursuit of short-term gains, decisions that often came at the expense of the very values he now sought to uphold.

"Jake, you're at a crossroads," he told himself as he stared out of his office window, his mind a whirlwind of introspection. He began to sift through his memories, replaying decisions he had made in the heat of the moment—decisions that compromised the very values he wanted to uphold. He recalled the times he had prioritized short-term gains over long-term integrity, allowing ego and ambition to overshadow the principles he held dear. A pang of remorse gnawed at him as he realized the potential harm these decisions caused to the company's culture and his own sense of Honor. "Can I truly lead this transformation?" he wondered, questioning his own capacity to change.

The next morning, Jake found himself sitting across from Maddy in a quiet corner of the coffee shop, his demeanor a mix of vulnerability and determination. "Maddy, I've been doing some deep introspection," he admitted, his voice tinged with honesty. Maddy looked at him with a reassuring smile. "Jake, that's an essential step in this journey. It's not just about transforming the company's culture—it's about personal growth as well." Jake nodded, his gaze fixed on his coffee cup. "I've been replaying past decisions in my mind, decisions that I know contradicted the very principles I want to promote now. I can't help but feel regret for compromising my values." Maddy's gaze softened, understanding his internal struggle. "Jake, we're all human, and growth involves acknowledging our past mistakes. The fact that you're reflecting on your decisions shows your commitment to change." Jake sighed, his shoulders relaxing as he absorbed her words. "But can I really lead this transformation? Can I ask others to change when I myself have faltered?" Maddy leaned forward, her eyes meeting his with sincerity. "Jake, leadership isn't about perfection; it's about growth and learning from our mistakes. Your vulnerability in acknowledging your past choices will resonate with your team. It will show them that you're willing to change and that you believe in the journey toward high Honor." Jake met her gaze, his resolve strengthening. "I want to be that leader—the one who guides the transformation and walks the path of change." Maddy nodded, a glimmer of pride in her eyes. "Jake, the fact that you're asking these questions and having these conversations is proof that you're already on the right path. Embrace this journey with genuine commitment to growth, and you'll inspire others to do the same."

In this intimate dialogue between Jake and Maddy, Jake's inner turmoil and vulnerability come to the forefront. Through candid conversations, he begins to grapple with his past decisions and seek a path of personal growth and transformation. Maddy's guidance provides him with the assurance and inspiration he needs to lead both himself and his organization toward a culture of high Honor.

Jake recognized that the journey toward high Honor was a personal one as much as it was organizational. He acknowledged the responsibility that came with his leadership role and the impact his decisions could have on the entire ecosystem of Danalgo.

The transformation was palpable in the interactions among the leaders. What was once a terrain of competition and ego-driven agendas began to shift. Transparency replaced secrecy, and collaboration replaced isolation. The concept of core values took center stage, guiding decisions, actions, and interactions. The leaders began to see themselves as stewards of a legacy, entrusted with the responsibility of shaping a culture that valued Honor above all else.

In one poignant moment, a Division Leader, Maria Lopez, stood before her peers and recounted an incident from her past. She shared how, in the pursuit of a business deal, she had overlooked the environmental impact of a manufacturing process. The result had been disastrous, causing harm to the community and the environment. Her voice trembled as she acknowledged her past choices, her voice cracking with emotion as she expressed her commitment to never repeat such mistakes. Her vulnerability rang true with the entire room, igniting a collective sense of empathy and determination.

The change was further underscored by the emergence of a collective code of ethics, crafted by the leaders themselves. This code outlined a commitment to transparency, Honorable decision-making, and the well-being of all stakeholders. The leaders recognized that their actions had ripple effects that extended beyond the confines of the organization—a realization that deepened their dedication to the journey of high Honor.

However, amidst the transformation, a shadow loomed. Blaine DeShield, Danalgo's Chief Operating Officer, remained obstinate in his resistance to change. Blaine saw the HONOR project as a threat to his own aspirations of becoming CEO. He believed that by derailing the project and undermining Jake's efforts, he could secure his own ascent to power. Blaine's scheming cast a cloud of tension over the organization, a tension that threatened to derail the progress that had been made.

As the leaders continued their journey from self-centeredness to values-driven leadership, the stakes grew higher. The battle between Honor and self-interest intensified, as each leader grappled with their own inner demons and their collective commitment to a better way of leading. The journey was far from over, and the challenges that lay ahead were as formidable as they were transformative.

Reflections 3-2-1

Lessons Learned: In this chapter, the concept of transforming business leaders from self-centeredness to values-driven leadership was explored. We learned that this transformation involves a deep introspection into past decisions, vulnerabilities, and a commitment to personal growth.

Key Takeaways:

1. **Embracing Vulnerability:** Leaders must confront their past decisions, even those that contradicted their values, with honesty and vulnerability. Acknowledging mistakes is a crucial step towards transformation.

2. **Leadership Growth:** Leadership isn't about perfection but about continuous growth. Acknowledging past errors and committing to change demonstrates authenticity and inspires others.

3. **Shared Responsibility:** Leaders have a collective responsibility to shape a culture of Honor. Their decisions resonate beyond the organization, emphasizing the significance of Honorable decision-making.

Reflective Questions:

1. **Compromise:** Can you recall a past decision that compromised your values? How could acknowledging it contribute to your growth as a leader?

2. **Reconciliation:** What does leadership growth mean to you? How do you envision reconciling your past choices with your commitment to change?

Compelling Action Step:

1. **Embrace Vulnerability:** Engage in open conversations with your team about your past mistakes and the lessons you've learned. Vulnerability can inspire a culture of trust and growth.

As we delve into the transformation of business leaders from self-centeredness to values-driven leadership, we recognize the power of self-awareness and vulnerability. The journey isn't linear; it involves confronting our past choices, acknowledging shortcomings, and committing to change. By taking these steps, we pave the way for personal growth and inspire a culture of Honor that extends beyond ourselves. The challenges are significant, but the rewards—a more Honorable, purpose-driven form of leadership—are immeasurable.

Chapter 4: Community Leaders
Bridging Divides and Building Unity

Amidst the tumultuous journey of transformation, a new chapter unfolded—one that explored the role of leaders in the broader community. These were not just leaders within the confines of Danalgo; they were individuals who held sway over neighborhoods, constituencies, and social circles. Their actions reverberated far beyond the boardrooms and offices of the organization.

As the leaders ventured into the realm of community engagement, they encountered a landscape fraught with challenges and complexities. The call to bridge divides and build unity was not just a lofty ideal—it was a call to action, a summons to engage with the very fabric of society. The leaders needed to transcend their own preconceptions and biases, learning to actively listen, empathize, and address the concerns of the communities they served.

At the heart of this transition was a recognition that community leaders were not just wielders of power, but stewards of collective well-being. Their decisions had far-reaching implications for the lives of individuals and families who depended on them for guidance and support. The journey of high Honor demanded that they look beyond their immediate interests and truly understand the needs of the people they were entrusted to lead.

Jake McLeash, CEO of Danalgo, found himself grappling with the challenge of community engagement. The transformation he was driving within the organization had far-reaching effects, and he realized that the principles of The HONOR Code needed to extend beyond the company's walls. As he stepped into the role of a community leader, he encountered a diverse array of concerns and aspirations that went beyond the balance sheets and bottom lines.

In one poignant interaction, Jake met with a group of local residents who expressed concerns about the environmental impact of Danalgo's operations.

Jake: Good afternoon, everyone. Thank you for taking the time to meet with me today. Your concerns about the environmental impact of our operations are important, and I'm here to listen and understand.

Mrs. Archer: Thank you, Mr. McLeash. We've been living here for generations, and we've seen the changes in our environment. We worry about the pollution and how it's affecting our health and the well-being of our children.

Jake: I truly appreciate your honesty. Your worries are valid, and I want you to know that we're committed to addressing them. Can you share more about the specific issues you've observed?

Mr. Haley: Well, our water used to be crystal clear, and now it's not safe to swim or fish in some areas. The air quality has also worsened, and we fear for the long-term consequences.

Jake: I understand how important these issues are to your community. Please know that we take your concerns seriously. We're already in the process of reviewing our operations and assessing their impact on the environment. But beyond that, I'd like to explore how we can work together to find solutions.

Mr. Groves: We've felt unheard for so long. It's reassuring to hear you say that. But how can we trust that this isn't just lip service?

Jake: That's a fair question, and I understand your skepticism. Building trust takes time, and it's not something that can happen overnight. But I'm committed to transparency and accountability. I'll personally ensure that our efforts to address these environmental concerns are shared with your community, and I invite you to hold us accountable for the actions we take.

Mrs. Fuentes: It's a step in the right direction, but we want to be part of the decision-making process too. Our lives are intertwined with this land, and we want to have a say in its future.

Jake: Your involvement is crucial. We're in this together, and I believe that collaboration is the key to finding sustainable solutions. I'd like to propose forming a community advisory board where you can voice your opinions, share your insights, and actively participate in shaping our environmental initiatives. Your perspective is invaluable, and I want to ensure it's taken into account.

Mrs. Archer: That sounds promising, Mr. McLeash. But can we really make a difference?

Jake: Absolutely. Change begins with collective action. By working together, we can make a positive impact on our environment and the well-being of everyone here. Let's take this opportunity to transform our concerns into solutions, our frustrations into action.

In this interaction, Jake demonstrates his genuine commitment to listening, understanding, and collaborating with the local residents. He acknowledges their concerns, assures them of his dedication, and proposes a concrete way forward that involves their active participation. This dialogue fosters trust, opens lines of communication, and highlights Jake's sincere desire to address the environmental impact of Danalgo's operations.

Rather than dismiss their concerns or minimize their grievances, Jake chose a different path. He listened intently, engaging in a dialogue that transcended corporate jargon and touched the heart of the matter.

Through active listening and empathetic engagement, Jake began to bridge the gap between the organization and the community. He acknowledged their concerns, took their perspectives into consideration, and initiated steps to address the environmental issues raised. His actions were not driven by a desire to merely placate, but by a genuine commitment to align the organization's operations with the values of Honor and integrity.

As the other leaders followed suit, a transformational shift occurred in the way community leaders interacted with their constituencies. Division Leaders, who had once disregarded community needs, now embarked on initiatives that contributed to uplifting local neighborhoods. Department Heads, who had been insulated from the concerns of the wider society, now actively sought input from those affected by their decisions.

The journey was not without its challenges. The leaders faced resistance from within and outside the organization, and the process of building unity proved to be arduous. However, high Honor acted as a guiding light, propelling them forward in the face of adversity. The realization that their actions had the power to create positive change, not just within Danalgo but in the broader community, fueled their determination.

The leaders of Danalgo are navigating the complexities of community engagement. They are learning that being a community leader means more than holding a title—it means actively participating in the lives of those they serve, understanding their needs, and working tirelessly to bridge divides and build unity.

Leaders' Empathetic Engagement

In the ever-expanding tapestry of their transformation, the leaders of Danalgo found themselves at a critical juncture—immersing themselves in the art of empathetic engagement with the communities they served. No longer content to be distant figures wielding influence from afar, they embarked on a journey to listen, learn, and understand.

Maria Lopez, a Division Leader, stood as a beacon of this new approach. In her role, she oversaw a manufacturing division that had often been at odds with the neighboring residential community due to environmental concerns. Armed with the principles of high Honor, Maria initiated a series of town hall meetings where residents were invited to voice their grievances and share their experiences.

With a genuine desire to understand, Maria listened as stories were shared—the tales of children suffering from respiratory issues, of families struggling with contaminated water, of dreams marred by the shadows of pollution. Maria's heart swelled with empathy as she absorbed the pain and frustration of those whose lives had been directly impacted by her division's operations.

As the leaders were doing within the organization, Maria applied the pillar of Reflection to her interactions with the community. She confronted the uncomfortable truths of her division's past decisions, acknowledging their shortcomings and the ways in which they fell short of upholding the values of Honor. Through this self-assessment, she was able to craft a vision for change—a vision that placed the well-being of the community at its core.

The transformation was not solely driven by town hall meetings and dialogues; it extended to tangible actions. Maria collaborated with environmental experts to devise strategies for reducing the division's impact on the community. She rallied her team to implement sustainable practices that aligned with the values of high Honor. It wasn't just about profit margins anymore; it was about creating a legacy of positive change for generations to come.

Maria's example inspired others to follow suit. The leaders of Danalgo learned that empathetic engagement was not a one-time gesture, but a continuous commitment. They began to see the community not as an external entity, but as an integral part of the ecosystem they were entrusted to nurture. The pillars of Others-Focus and Reflection became guiding principles, guiding them to actively consider the implications of their decisions on the lives of those they served.

The skepticism that had once clouded their engagement with the community began to dissipate, replaced by a genuine desire to bridge divides and build unity. The transformation was not easy—it demanded vulnerability, humility, and an openness to change. But with Maddy Davidson's guidance, the leaders of Danalgo were forging a new path—one that prioritized empathy, collaboration, and the well-being of the community.

The leaders continue their journey of empathetic engagement with the community. They are learning that the role of a leader transcends personal ambitions and corporate objectives—it is a role that demands a commitment to the well-being and unity of the community they serve.

Prioritizing Community Well-Being

As the leaders of Danalgo continued to navigate the path of transformation, a shift occurred within their perspectives. The transition from self-centeredness to others-focus leadership took root, transforming their priorities and inspiring them to champion the well-being of the community over personal interests.

Jake McLeash, CEO of Danalgo, found himself at the forefront of this transition. His interactions with the community revealed the stark reality of the impact his decisions could have on the lives of individuals. What were once distant statistics and abstract considerations were now imbued with faces, stories, and dreams.

Jake's journey took him to the doorstep of a single mother who had lost her job due to environmental pollution caused by Danalgo's operations.

Jake: Good afternoon. I appreciate you taking the time to meet with me today.

Mom: Thank you for coming. My name's Emily. Please come in.

Jake: Thank you, Emily. I'm Jake McLeash, the CEO of Danalgo. I wanted to talk to you personally about the challenges you've been facing.

Emily: It's been really hard. I lost my job at the local factory because of the pollution. It was the only source of income for my family.

Jake: I'm truly sorry to hear that. Your situation is exactly what I want to address. I want to understand the impact our operations have had on you and your family.

Emily: It's not just about my job. My daughter has been having health issues, and I can't help but think it's connected to the air and water quality here.

Jake: Your daughter's health is a priority, and I can't imagine how difficult this must be for you. Please know that I'm committed to making things right.

Emily: It's not just about making things right now. We need to ensure that this doesn't happen to anyone else in the future. Our community deserves a safe and healthy environment.

Jake: You're absolutely right, Emily. Our responsibility extends beyond just fixing immediate issues. We need to ensure a sustainable future for everyone. That's why I'm determined to address the root causes of the pollution and find lasting solutions.

Emily: I appreciate your words, Mr. McLeash, but words alone won't change our situation. I need to know that you're serious about this.

Jake: I understand your skepticism, and I'm here to show you that I'm serious about change. We're already working on reducing our environmental footprint, and I want your input on how we can do better. I'm committed to involving the community in the decision-making process.

Emily: That's a step in the right direction, but it's going to take a lot to regain our trust. My daughter's health is at stake, and I won't back down until I'm sure things are improving.

Jake: I respect your determination, Emily. Rebuilding trust takes time, but I'm dedicated to earning it back. Your daughter's health and the well-being of our community are at the forefront of my priorities.

Emily: I hope so, Mr. McLeash. This isn't just about business decisions; it's about people's lives. I hope you understand that.

Jake: I do understand, Emily. Meeting you and hearing your story has reinforced the fact that the impact of our operations goes far beyond numbers on a balance sheet. It's about real people with real lives, and I take that responsibility seriously.

Emily: I'll be watching to see if your actions match your words. Our community deserves better.

Jake: You have my word that I'll do everything in my power to make a positive change. Thank you for sharing your story with me, Emily. It's given me a renewed sense of purpose.

This conversation between Jake and Emily showcases Jake's genuine concern for the individuals affected by the environmental pollution caused by Danalgo's operations. He listens empathetically to her struggles, acknowledges his responsibilities as a leader, and expresses his commitment to meaningful change. Emily's candidness reminds him of the personal stakes involved and strengthens his resolve to prioritize the community's well-being.

As he listened to her struggles, he realized the weight of his responsibilities as a leader. The well-being of the community wasn't just an abstract concept; it was a tangible reality that he had the power to influence.

Driven by this realization, Jake began to prioritize community well-being in every facet of his decision-making. The choices he made weren't solely about profit margins; they were about ensuring that the community thrived alongside the organization. The pillar of Non-Negotiables, which emphasized unwavering principles regardless of circumstances, guided his commitment to upholding the highest standards of Honorable conduct.

Jake's journey was echoed by the other leaders within Danalgo. Division Leaders initiated philanthropic initiatives to address pressing community needs. Department Heads explored partnerships with local organizations to enhance education and healthcare opportunities. The shift from self-centeredness to prioritizing the well-being of the community became a unifying thread that wove through the fabric of the organization.

The concept of high Honor became more than a buzzword; it was a living, breathing force that shaped their decisions, actions, and interactions. The transformation was not just organizational—it was cultural. The leaders recognized that they held a responsibility to foster an environment where Honor was not just an aspiration, but a lived reality that permeated every level of leadership.

The leaders of Danalgo have learned to place the well-being of the community at the forefront of their priorities. They are embracing the transformation from self-centeredness to others-focus leadership, driven by the conviction that their actions can create positive change that reverberates beyond the organization's walls.

Reflections 3-2-1

Lessons Learned: Throughout this chapter, we delved into the concept of leaders as community stewards, moving beyond self-centeredness to prioritize the well-being of the larger ecosystem. We learned that community engagement isn't a mere buzzword, but a tangible commitment that requires empathy, transparency, and collaboration.

Key Takeaways:

1. **Broader Impact:** The actions of leaders have far-reaching consequences that extend beyond their organizations. Leaders are not just wielders of power but stewards of collective well-being.

2. **Empathetic Engagement:** Engaging with the community demands active listening, genuine understanding, and a commitment to collaborate on solutions. Leaders must address concerns with sincerity and transparency.

3. **Community Well-Being:** Prioritizing the well-being of the community is a fundamental responsibility of leaders. This involves transcending personal interests and making decisions that align with the values of Honor and integrity.

Reflective Questions:

1. **Longer Term:** Have I considered the broader impact of my decisions beyond immediate results? How can I prioritize long-term community well-being?

2. **Build Bridges:** What steps can I take to bridge divides and build unity within my sphere of influence, whether in my organization or community?

Compelling Action Steps:

1. **Initiate Dialogue:** Engage in open dialogues with community members to understand their concerns and aspirations. Actively listen and involve them in shaping solutions.

The leaders of Danalgo have embarked on a transformation—navigating the complexities of community engagement, prioritizing the well-being of others, and striving to bridge divides. The journey has required vulnerability, humility, and a genuine commitment to change. As they embrace the principles of high Honor, these leaders are not just shaping their organization, but also inspiring a culture of unity and positive change that extends far beyond their corporate walls.

Chapter 5: Government Leaders:
Upholding Democracy and Responsibility

In the sprawling landscape of transformation, the spotlight shifted to a new set of leaders—those entrusted with the responsibility of governance and the stewardship of democracy. Government Leaders, who had often been marred by allegations of corruption and ethical lapses, found themselves at a crossroads. The journey that awaited them was one of great change, a shift from engaging in corruption to championing transparency and accountability.

As the narrative unfolded, the story of the local and state Government Leaders responsible that represented the areas Danalgo is located became a reflection of the broader challenges facing governance in modern society. The lines between personal interests and public service were often blurred, and the consequences of such blurred lines rippled through communities, eroding trust and perpetuating a culture of cynicism.

Enter Jake McLeash, CEO of Danalgo, who embarked on a transformational journey within his organization and was now determined to extend the principles of high Honor to the realm of government. Armed with the guidance of Maddy Davidson, he found himself at the epicenter of a movement to redefine the relationship between leadership and integrity.

Jake's efforts were not met without resistance. The government leaders he sought to influence were deeply entrenched in a system where corruption had become normalized. The battle to champion transparency and accountability was an uphill one, as the allure of personal gain often clouded the path to Honorable conduct.

One of the pivotal moments occurred during a meeting of city council members. The issue at hand was a proposed infrastructure project that promised personal gains for certain council members through underhanded dealings. Jake, as an outsider in the realm of politics, faced the daunting task of challenging the status quo and rallying the leaders toward a higher standard.

With conviction and determination, Jake shared the lessons he learned through the journey of high Honor. He reminded them that their role was not just to represent themselves, but the well-being of the entire community. He implored them to consider the impact of their decisions on the lives of ordinary citizens who entrusted them with their voices.

Jake had a series of meetings with the council members in their offices. His last meeting was with Council Member Harris.

Council Member Harris: Ah, Jake McLeash, CEO of Danalgo. What brings you to my office today?

Jake: Thank you for seeing me, Council Member Harris. I've come to discuss the proposed infrastructure project that's currently on the table.

Council Member Harris: Ah, that project. It's a golden opportunity for progress and development, don't you think?

Jake: I do understand the desire for progress, Council Member Harris. But I have concerns about the way this project is being approached.

Council Member Harris: Concerns? We've done our due diligence. The benefits far outweigh any minor ethical concerns.

Jake: I appreciate your perspective, but I believe we must also consider the ethical implications. Our decisions as leaders have the power to shape lives, and I think it's crucial that we prioritize the well-being of the community above personal gains.

Council Member Harris: (leaning back) Well, Jake, sometimes tough decisions have to be made. We can't always please everyone.

Jake: That's true, Council Member Harris. But the decisions we make should reflect the values we stand for. The journey I've been on within Danalgo has taught me that leadership isn't just about the bottom line—it's about creating a positive impact on people's lives.

Council Member Harris: (scoffs) Positive impact? We're talking about economic growth, job opportunities!

Jake: And those are important, absolutely. But we can achieve growth and opportunities without compromising our integrity. What legacy are we leaving behind for future generations if our decisions are clouded by self-interest?

Council Member Harris: (leaning forward) Look, Jake, I appreciate your concern, but you're new to this game. Politics is about negotiation, compromise.

Jake: (firmly) I understand that, Council Member Harris. But compromise shouldn't mean sacrificing our values. Our constituents trust us to represent their best interests. Shouldn't that be our guiding principle?

Council Member Harris: (pauses) You're an idealist, Jake. This is how things work in the real world.

Jake: I don't believe that we have to accept a flawed status quo. We have the power to change things for the better. It starts with making choices that align with our values, even when it's challenging.

Council Member Harris: (sighs) You're asking a lot, Jake.

Jake: I'm asking for us to rise above personal interests and prioritize the greater good. Imagine the impact we could have if we lead with integrity and Honor. The community would thrive, and we would leave a legacy we could be proud of.

Council Member Harris: (reflects for a moment) You've given me something to think about, Jake. This isn't an easy decision.

Jake: I understand, Council Member Harris. It's not about making easy decisions; it's about making the right ones. I believe we can make a difference together.

Council Member Harris: (nods) Well, you've certainly given me a lot to consider. I appreciate your perspective, even if it challenges the norm.

Jake: Thank you for taking the time to listen, Council Member Harris. I believe in the potential for positive change, even in the realm of politics.

Council Member Harris: We'll see, Jake. Change is never as simple as it sounds.

Jake: It may not be simple, but it's worth striving for. Our leadership has the power to inspire others and create a better future.

It was a tense yet meaningful interaction between Jake and Council Member Harris. Jake's Honorable leadership and his willingness to challenge the status quo is evident as he navigates a complex political landscape. The conversation highlights the clash between personal gains and community well-being, emphasizing the importance of values-driven decision-making in leadership.

As the council members deliberated, the lines between personal interests and public responsibility began to blur. The weight of their choices bore heavily on their shoulders, and they found themselves at a crossroads. The journey of transformation had begun, as these Government Leaders confronted the ethical quagmire they were entangled in.

Jake's efforts were supported by Samantha Knight, his mentor and staunch advocate on the Danalgo board of directors. Samantha's wisdom and experience provided the moral compass that these leaders desperately needed. Through candid conversations and thought-provoking insights, she guided them toward a renewed commitment to integrity and Honorable conduct.

These Government Leaders are at the precipice of change. They are faced with the challenge of transitioning from a culture of corruption to one of transparency and accountability. Their journey is fraught with obstacles, but it is a journey that has the potential to reshape their roles in governance and the very essence of democracy itself.

Navigating Legal and Ethical Boundaries

The transition of Danalgo's Government Leaders from engaging in corruption to championing transparency and accountability was a journey fraught with challenges. As these leaders embarked on the path of change, they found themselves facing instances that required them to navigate the complex interplay between legal mandates and ethical imperatives.

One such instance involved a proposed zoning change that had the potential to benefit a select group of individuals at the expense of the wider community. The issue was marked by layers of complexity, as the leaders were forced to grapple with the fine line between pursuing personal gain and upholding the principles of transparency and the public interest.

Jake McLeash, CEO of Danalgo, found himself at the center of this ethical quandary as he collaborated with the Government

Leaders. Drawing from the lessons of high Honor, he urged them to consider the broader implications of their choices on the community they served. He encouraged them to prioritize the well-being of the many over the interests of the few.

As discussions unfolded, the Government Leaders were confronted with the ethical dilemma of maximizing transparency while adhering to the bounds of legality.

Deputy Mayor: Hello?

Council Member Wiggins: Hey, it's me. Let's talk about the upcoming vote.

Deputy Mayor Carvallo: Sure thing. We've got a big call to make.

Council Member Wiggins: Yeah, the project could boost the economy, but the environmental impact is worrying.

Deputy Mayor Carvallo: I've been wrestling with that too. Economy matters, but we can't ignore the environment.

Council Member Wiggins: True, but turning this down might cost us opportunities.

Deputy Mayor Carvallo: I Reflected on this. My Non-Negotiables and Others-Focus tell us we can't let short-term gains sway us. People voted us in to look out for their best interests.

Council Member Wiggins: It's a tightrope walk.

Deputy Mayor Carvallo: Agreed. Let's channel the HONOR Code. We need a solution that's Honorable and responsible.

Council Member Wiggins: Tough task ahead.

DM: It won't be simple, but that's leadership. We need a decision we can stand by, even if it's tough.

Council Member Wiggins: You're right. We've got to think long-term.

Deputy Mayor Carvallo: Our constituents and our own principles are at stake.

Council Member Wiggins: Alright, let's dive into the options and find that balance.

Deputy Mayor Carvallo: Agreed. Let's aim for progress without sacrificing responsibility.

They recognized that their decisions had the potential to set a precedent for Honorable conduct in governance, rippling far beyond their immediate jurisdiction. The lessons of the HONOR Code guided them as they sought solutions that upheld the values of integrity and responsibility.

Maddy Davidson, the Guide who led the transformation within Danalgo, played a pivotal role in guiding the Government Leaders through the intricate web of legal and ethical considerations.

Maddy: Good morning, Deputy Mayor Carvallo. Thank you for taking the time to meet.

Deputy Mayor (Carvallo): Of course, Maddy. Your insights have been invaluable throughout this journey.

Maddy: I'm glad to be of help. The ethical complexities that government leaders face can be quite challenging.

Carvallo: You're telling me. Balancing progress and responsibility isn't as straightforward as it seems.

Maddy: Indeed. Take the upcoming project vote, for instance. It's crucial to consider both economic benefits and environmental impact.

Carvallo: That's the heart of the matter. We want growth, but not at the cost of our community's well-being.

Maddy: Absolutely. And that's where the lessons from Danalgo's transformation come into play. The HONOR Code emphasizes values-driven decisions even when they're tough.

Carvallo: It sounds great in theory, but real-world politics can be messy.

Maddy: I understand the challenges. But the legacy we leave behind is shaped by the decisions we make now.

Carvallo: You're right. We can't let short-term gains blind us to the long-term impact.

Maddy: And that's where transparency comes in. If we communicate the reasons behind our decisions, people are more likely to understand.

Carvallo: Agreed. But how do we navigate the legal boundaries?

Maddy: It's about pushing for innovative solutions that align with both ethics and regulations. Finding that middle ground is where true leadership shines.

Carvallo: It's not going to be easy, Maddy. There will be pressures from all sides.

Maddy: True leadership often means standing firm in the face of challenges. Remember, your role is to serve the community's best interests.

Carvallo: You're right. It's not about personal gains, but about the well-being of the people we represent.

Maddy: Precisely. And remember, Deputy Mayor, you're not alone in this. Your fellow leaders share the same journey.

Carvallo: Your guidance has been a compass for us, Maddy. Thank you for reminding me of our responsibilities.

Maddy: It's been my privilege to guide you all. Let's work together to find a solution that upholds integrity and progress.

Carvallo: Let's do it. Our community deserves nothing less.

Her expertise helped them navigate the delicate balance between the demands of their positions and the call to serve the public good.

In another instance, the leaders found themselves at odds with a proposed budget allocation that allocated funds to pet projects while neglecting critical community needs. Samantha Knight, Jake's mentor and advocate on the Danalgo board, provided sage counsel that echoed the principles of high Honor. She reminded them that leadership wasn't just about maintaining positions of power; it was about fostering an environment where transparency was upheld as a foundational value.

Through introspection, collaboration, and principled decision-making, the Government Leaders began to find ways to optimize transparency without compromising their ethical commitments. They engaged in candid conversations with their constituents, explaining the complexities of their decisions and the rationale behind their choices. They recognized that transparency wasn't just about sharing information—it was about fostering trust and accountability.

The Government Leaders are navigating the intricacies of Honorable decision-making within the realm of governance. They are discovering that transparency and the public interest can coexist, and that their choices have the power to shape their immediate circumstances and the broader landscape of democracy and responsibility.

A Covenant with the Public Interest

The journey of the Government Leaders whose constituents were Danalgo employees and their neighbors was not just about changing their approach to governance—it was about embracing a commitment to serve the public interest and uphold the very bedrock of democratic values. As they navigated the complex terrain of Honorable decisions, their dedication to the well-being of the community became a rallying cry that echoed through the corridors of power.

With a renewed sense of purpose, the Government Leaders began to implement a series of changes aimed at maximizing transparency, accountability, and integrity. They recognized that their positions were not vehicles for personal enrichment, but platforms for enacting positive change that transcended their own interests. Their choices were guided by the non-negotiable principles of high Honor that demanded steadfast truth and justice.

One of the most pivotal moments occurred during a town hall meeting where Mayor Marinez engaged directly with constituents. In a display of humility and transparency, She openly shared the challenges they had faced, the ethical dilemmas they had navigated, and the transformational journey they were embarking upon.

Mayor Martinez: Ladies and gentlemen, thank you for joining us today. This town hall meeting is of utmost importance as we come together to discuss decisions that will shape the pursuit of Honor in our community.

Our aim has always been to make choices that reflect the Honor we hold dear. Yet, let's be frank – the path to progress is often complicated. We've encountered ethical dilemmas that have tested our commitment to both development and the principles we stand for.

There's a transformation taking place within our leadership, grounded in the values of the HONOR Code. This journey hasn't been effortless; it's required us to face uncomfortable truths about our past decisions.

Transparency has become our guiding light. Sharing our journey with you isn't about seeking validation; it's about demonstrating our dedication to the democratic principles that bind us together. Your voices have been entrusted to us, and we're committed to ensuring they are heard and genuinely Honored.

We've come together to discuss the intricacies of policies, to balance growth with sustainability, and tread the fine line between legality and ethical responsibility. These discussions have been robust, sometimes marked by differing opinions, but always united by a shared pursuit of Honor – to serve you, our community.

Today, we stand before you not as distant figures, but as individuals who are integral parts of this community. We face the same challenges and yearn for the same brighter future. We are here to listen, understand, and work together towards an Honor-filled path.

Thank you for your trust. Thank you for holding us accountable. Let this mark the start of a new chapter in our community's heritage – a chapter where Honor, ethics, and progress are not merely words, but the very essence of our actions.

This transparency wasn't just an act—it was a testament to their commitment to uphold democratic values and ensure that the voices of the people they served were heard.

Samantha Knight emphasized the importance of fostering a culture of accountability. She encouraged the Government Leaders to hold themselves to the highest standards of conduct and to be willing to course-correct when necessary. Her guidance echoed the principles of the HONOR Code, where the pillars of Reflection and Non-Negotiables served as guiding lights for responsible governance.

The Government Leaders began to collaborate with civic organizations and experts to implement measures that would prevent corruption, enhance transparency, and strengthen democratic institutions. They championed initiatives that empowered citizens to actively participate in decision-making processes, making democracy a lived reality rather than a mere concept. The commitment to the public interest was no longer a theoretical notion; it was a covenant that drove their actions.

The transformation was not without challenges. The leaders faced resistance from those who sought to maintain the status quo, as well as internal struggles as they grappled with their own vulnerabilities and biases. However, the lessons of high Honor provided them with a compass to navigate these obstacles, reminding them that the pursuit of the greater good was a journey worth undertaking.

Through Danalgo's influence, these Government Leaders immersed themselves in a transformative journey that goes beyond individual ambitions. They are committed to serving the public interest and upholding democratic values that transcend personal gain. They are guided by Honor, integrity, and a pledge to the principles that underpin the fabric of society.

Reflections 3-2-1

Lessons Learned: In this chapter, we explored the concept of Honorable transformation within the realm of government leadership. We learned that transitioning from corruption to transparency requires navigating complex ethical dilemmas and prioritizing the public interest over personal gains.

Key Takeaways:

1. **Ethical Complexity:** The journey of Government Leaders toward Honorable governance highlighted the intricate web of ethical considerations that arise in the pursuit of transparency and accountability.

2. **Balancing Interests:** The challenge of balancing economic growth with environmental responsibility underscores the necessity of principled decision-making that aligns with the values of the HONOR Code.

3. **Transparent Leadership:** Transparency isn't just about sharing information; it's about fostering trust and accountability among constituents, demonstrating that decisions are made with their best Interests at heart.

Reflective Questions:

1. **Transparency:** In what ways can transparency be integrated into decision-making processes? How does transparent leadership contribute to building public trust?

2. **Considerations:** Reflect on a situation where you had to make a tough decision that impacted others. How did you balance personal interests with ethical considerations? What did you learn from the experience?

Compelling Action Steps:

1. **Promote Civic Engagement:** Create platforms for citizen participation in decision-making, fostering a sense of ownership and accountability among the community.

We recognize that Honorable transformation within government leadership is not a destination but an ongoing journey. Upholding democracy and responsibility requires a commitment to values that transcend individual ambitions, prioritizing the collective well-being of the community. The lessons learned from these Government Leaders serve as a testament to the potential for positive change when leaders choose to champion integrity, transparency, and the pursuit of Honor.

Chapter 6: The Ripple Effect

A Tapestry of Transformation

The transformation that was set in motion by the leaders of Danalgo was far from confined to the confines of their own journeys—it began to weave its way through the very fabric of their sectors and the organization as a whole. The ripple effect of the principles of high Honor began to echo outward, touching lives and reshaping the landscape of leadership, families, and culture.

In the realm of Government Leaders, the impact was palpable. The once-disheartened constituents who had lost faith in their representatives found themselves inspired by a new era of transparency and accountability. Town hall meetings were no longer mere formalities; they were platforms for meaningful dialogue and genuine engagement. Citizens began to recognize that their voices mattered and that their leaders were committed to serving their interests.

The transformation extended to the broader community as well. As Government Leaders championed initiatives that upheld the public interest, the community responded with a renewed sense of unity and collaboration. Civic organizations, previously skeptical of government intentions, found themselves partnering with leaders to drive positive change. The community's well-being was no longer a passive consideration—it was a shared responsibility that flowed through every level of society.

Similarly, in the realm of Business Leaders, the transformation sparked a cultural shift within Danalgo. The principles of high Honor became embedded in the organization's DNA, guiding decisions, interactions, and strategic initiatives. The focus on core values and Honorable conduct culminated in a shift toward a values-driven approach to business. As leaders embraced transparency and accountability, employee morale soared, and a sense of purpose permeated the workplace.

Jake McLeash, CEO of Danalgo, had become a symbol of this transformation. His commitment to the HONOR Code catalyzed a cascade of positive change, demonstrating that Honorable leadership was a force for good beyond financial success. The ripple effect of his journey was evident in the renewed dedication of his team, the innovative approaches to problem-solving, and the organic growth of a culture founded on Honor and integrity.

The impact also extended beyond the organization's walls to the families of the employees. As employees experienced personal growth and fulfillment within a values-driven environment, they carried those values back to their homes. The principles of high Honor were woven into the tapestry of family life, fostering connections built on empathy, respect, and an Others-Focus.

The leaders of Danalgo stand in awe of the transformative power of their journey. The ripple effect of the HONOR Code has touched lives, reshaped institutions, and ignited a movement that is larger than themselves. The fabric of leadership, families, and culture has been rewoven with threads of Honor, integrity, and a shared positive change.

Stay tuned for the next section of Chapter 6, where we'll highlight the positive changes in organizational culture, employee engagement, and stakeholder relationships. The impact of the leaders' transformations will come into focus, revealing a portrait of an organization that has risen to new heights of success through the power of high Honor.

A Flourishing Ecosystem of Honor

The transformative journey embarked upon by the leaders of Danalgo blossomed into a flourishing ecosystem of Honor that extended its tendrils into every facet of the organization. The positive changes in organizational culture, employee engagement, and stakeholder relationships were not mere anecdotes—they were the markers of a shift that reshaped the very essence of Danalgo's identity.

Organizational culture underwent a metamorphosis. The principles of the HONOR Code became embedded in the DNA of the organization, guiding the behaviors, decisions, and interactions of every employee. Collaboration and teamwork were no longer aspirational goals; they were the foundation upon which innovative ideas and solutions were built. The once-fragmented departments evolved into a cohesive unit, united by a shared Honor and integrity.

Employee engagement reached new heights. The transformational journey ignited a sense of purpose and belonging among the employees. They were no longer mere cogs in a machine; they were integral contributors to a mission that transcended profit margins. The focus on Others-Focus fostered an environment of support, empathy, and mutual respect. Employees felt seen, heard, and valued—an essential ingredient in their engagement and motivation.

Stakeholder relationships underwent a complete renaissance. The transparency and accountability did not go unnoticed by the partners, suppliers, and clients of Danalgo. Trust, once fragile and easily shattered, was replaced with a solid foundation built on the principles of high Honor. Stakeholders recognized that their interests were being actively considered and that their interactions with the organization were rooted in integrity.

Jake McLeash marveled at the positive changes that cascaded throughout the organization. The journey was not without its challenges, but the rewards were evident in every corner of the workplace. He witnessed a company that evolved from a place of transaction to a community of shared values and purpose.

Samantha Knight recognized the transformation as well. She noted that the ripple effect of the HONOR Code had far-reaching implications for the organization's reputation and public perception.

The positive changes in organizational culture, employee engagement, and stakeholder relationships stand as a testament to the power of Honor-driven leadership. The journey of transformation brought about individual growth and ushered in a new era of success for Danalgo—one defined by values, integrity, and serving the greater good.

A Beacon of Positive Change

The transformational journey undertaken by the leaders of Danalgo was noticed by the world at large. The improved public perception and reputation of the organization became a shining example of the potential for positive change when leaders commit to the principles of Honor and integrity.

As news of the organization's transformation spread, Danalgo began to earn the admiration and respect of its peers, competitors, and the general public. The once-cynical voices that had doubted the feasibility of Honorable leadership were silenced by the tangible results of Danalgo's journey. The organization was no longer seen solely as a profit-driven entity; it had become a beacon of positive change that inspired others to reconsider their own approaches to leadership.

Media outlets took notice, featuring stories that highlighted Danalgo's transformation as a case study in Honorable leadership. Interviews with Jake McLeash, Maddy Davidson, and other key figures in the organization's journey served as a source of inspiration for leaders across industries. The positive changes in organizational culture, employee engagement, and stakeholder relationships were showcased as evidence of the impact that high Honor could have on an organization's success.

Moreover, the improved reputation of Danalgo had tangible effects on its bottom line. Clients and partners were eager to collaborate with an organization that had a proven track record of Honorable conduct and transparency. The once-skeptical stakeholders became steadfast supporters, recognizing the value of aligning themselves with an organization that placed Honor at the forefront of its operations.

Jake McLeash found himself approached by industry conferences and events, eager to have him share his insights on Honorable leadership. The ripple effect of Danalgo's journey extended far beyond its walls, shaping conversations about the role of leadership in driving positive change. Jake, along with Maddy Davidson and Samantha Knight, became sought-after speakers and thought leaders in the realm of Honor-driven leadership.

The improved public perception and reputation of Danalgo stand as a testament to the transformative power of the HONOR Code. The journey of high Honor brought about internal change and inspired a movement that extended beyond the organization itself. Danalgo's story was no longer its own; it became a story of hope, possibility, and the potential for positive transformation in the realms of leadership, families, and culture.

The journey of transformation is not without its trials, and the leaders of Danalgo will learn that setbacks are opportunities for growth and further alignment with the principles of high Honor.

Reflections 3-2-1

Lessons Learned: In this chapter, we explored the ripple effect created by Honorable transformation within an organization. We learned that such transformation goes beyond individual journeys, influencing sectors, communities, families, and culture at large.

Key Takeaways:

1. **Ripple of Influence:** The commitment of leaders to Honorable values and the HONOR Code creates a ripple effect that extends far beyond their personal transformations, touching the lives of constituents, communities, and even influencing industry perceptions.

2. **Community Unity:** Transparency and accountability in governance inspire trust and unity among citizens, transforming town hall meetings into platforms for meaningful dialogue and engagement.

3. **Cultural Transformation:** Embracing the principles of high Honor redefines organizational culture, fostering collaboration, purpose-driven engagement, and strong stakeholder relationships.

Reflective Questions:

1. **Personal Honor:** Think about a time when a change in your personal values positively influenced your family or close relationships. How can this idea be applied to leadership and organizations?

2. **Influence:** Consider an organization or leader you admire for their Honorable practices. How might their positive influence extend beyond their immediate sphere of influence, echoing the ripple effect discussed in this chapter?

Compelling Action Steps:

1. **Embed Honor:** Integrate the core principles of high Honor into your organization's culture, allowing them to guide decision-making, interactions, and stakeholder relationships.

We recognize that the transformation within Danalgo illustrates the remarkable potential for Honorable leadership to ignite a ripple effect of positive change. The threads of high Honor have woven through leadership, communities, families, and culture, transcending individual achievements and inspiring a collective movement towards a more Honorable and accountable world. The impact of their journey continues to echo, reminding us that leadership has the power to be a catalyst for transformation beyond the boundaries of the self.

Chapter 7: Challenges and Setbacks
Embracing the Test of Resilience

The journey of transformation undertaken by the leaders of Danalgo was not without its share of challenges and setbacks. As they navigated the uncharted waters of Honor-driven leadership, they encountered obstacles that tested their resolve and demanded a deeper level of introspection and growth.

One of the most significant challenges emerged when the organization faced a sudden and unexpected financial crisis. External market forces created a downturn that threatened Danalgo's financial stability. The pressure to prioritize short-term financial gains clashed with the principles of the HONOR Code, creating a complex ethical dilemma. The leaders found themselves at a crossroads, forced to balance the organization's immediate financial needs with their Honor and integrity.

In the face of adversity, the lessons of high Honor provided a guiding light. Reflection became a critical tool as leaders paused to consider the long-term consequences of their decisions. Non-Negotiables, the unwavering principles that formed the bedrock of the HONOR Code, reminded them that upholding truth and integrity was non-negotiable, even in the face of financial strain. Their Others-Focus guided them to consider the impact of their choices on employees, stakeholders, and the community.

Samantha Knight played a pivotal role during this challenging period. Her support and guidance served as a reminder that Honorable leadership was not always the easiest path, but it was the right one. She encouraged the leaders to seek solutions that aligned with their values, even if they required short-term sacrifices.

The journey through setbacks illuminated the power of community and collaboration. The leaders of Danalgo found strength in their shared Honor. They engaged in open and honest discussions, recognizing that the solutions they sought needed to reflect the values they held dear. This collaboration wasn't just a practical strategy—it was an embodiment of the Others-Focus pillar of the HONOR Code.

The challenges and setbacks faced by the leaders of Danalgo serve as a testament to the complexities of Honor-driven leadership. Adversity tested their commitment to the principles of the HONOR Code, demanding resilience, introspection, and Honorable decision-making. Their journey through these challenges exemplified the transformation that occurs when leaders maintain their Honor despite adversity.

The journey of resilience and growth will reveal the depth of their dedication to positive transformation in leadership, families, and culture.

Upholding Honor in the Face of Adversity

The challenges and setbacks that tested the leaders of Danalgo also became a crucible for their Honor. As they navigated the stormy waters of adversity, their dedication to the principles of the HONOR Code served as a compass, guiding them through difficult decisions and complex dilemmas.

Blaine DeShield, the Chief Operating Officer, intensified his efforts to undermine the HONOR project as the organization faced challenges. His cunning maneuvers and manipulative tactics were aimed at derailing the transformational journey led by Jake McLeash and Maddy Davidson. Blaine's actions put a spotlight on the N pillar of the HONOR Code—Non-Negotiables. While he was willing to compromise values for personal gain, most of the leaders at Danalgo remained steady in their commitment to truth, integrity, empathy, and accountability.

The adversity presented the leaders with a litmus test of their transformation. As Blaine attempted to erode trust and unity within the organization, the leaders were called upon to demonstrate the principles of Others-Focus. Rather than retaliating with hostility, they chose to respond with empathy and acceptance. They engaged in open dialogues and sought to address concerns with compassion, fostering an environment of unity even in the face of division.

Samantha Knight's role as a mentor became even more crucial during these trying times. Her guidance and wisdom provided a steadying influence as the leaders navigated through the challenges. She reminded them that the journey of Honor was not linear—it was a path riddled with obstacles that required consistent reflection, growth, and the courage to stand up for what was right.

Their Honor was put to the test in every decision, interaction, and strategy crafted during this period. The leaders found themselves at a crossroads where their transformed behavior was challenged by the forces of adversity. However, they remained resolute, using Reflection to evaluate their choices, Others-Focus to consider the greater impact, and Non-Negotiables to uphold the unwavering principles that defined their journey.

The leaders of Danalgo showed that their transformation was not a mere facade—it was a fundamental shift that could withstand even the harshest trials. Their ability to maintain their commitment to Honor despite adversity demonstrated the depth of their growth and the authenticity of their journey.

Positive transformation has truly taken root, shaping their responses and decisions even in the face of seemingly insurmountable odds.

Strengthening the Foundation

As the leaders of Danalgo continued their journey, the challenges they faced served as opportunities to put their evolved behavior to the test. The principles of the HONOR Code, which became ingrained in their mindset as Habits, were put into action as they encountered situations that called for Honorable decision-making, empathy, and steadfast commitment.

One instance that highlighted their transformed behavior occurred during a critical negotiation with a key client. The negotiation process hit a roadblock, with both parties struggling to find common ground. In the past, this situation might have escalated into a battle of wills, focused solely on gaining the upper hand. However, the leaders now approached the negotiation with an Others-Focus perspective.

Instead of aiming for a win-lose outcome, the leaders sought a win-win solution that would benefit both parties. They actively listened to the client's concerns, empathized with their needs, and engaged in constructive dialogue. The approach of Others-Focus allowed them to build rapport and trust, paving the way for a mutually beneficial agreement. The transformation was evident in their ability to negotiate with integrity and collaboration.

In another instance, the organization faced a crisis related to a faulty product that had the potential to impact customer safety. The transformed leaders didn't shy away from accountability. Instead, they embraced Non-Negotiables and acted swiftly to address the issue. They took full responsibility, engaged in transparent communication with customers, and initiated a comprehensive recall and improvement plan. The crisis showcased their commitment to upholding truth, integrity, and empathy, even in the face of adversity.

Blaine DeShield's attempts to undermine the HONOR project also intensified during this period. His efforts to exploit weaknesses and sow discord within the organization tested the leaders' resilience and determination. However, their commitment to high Honor remained unshaken. They responded to his tactics with open communication, unity, and a focus on the values that had become their compass.

The leaders of Danalgo demonstrated that their transformed behavior was not just a theoretical concept—it was a practical and tangible reality. Their ability to navigate challenges while adhering to the principles of the HONOR Code showcased their readiness to face whatever tests came their way.

Has the HONOR Code truly become the foundation of their leadership, impacting their actions and the destiny of the organization itself?

Reflections 3-2-1

Lessons Learned: In this chapter, we dug into the challenges and setbacks that tested the leaders of Danalgo's commitment to the principles of the HONOR Code. We discovered that adversity serves as a crucible for growth, resilience, and the authentic application of transformed behaviors.

Key Takeaways:

1. **Resilience Amid Adversity:** The journey of transformation is not without its trials. Challenges become opportunities to put the principles of the HONOR Code into action, demonstrating the depth of commitment to ethical leadership.

2. **Navigating Ethical Dilemmas:** When faced with dilemmas that pit short-term gain against long-term values, leaders guided by high Honor engage in Reflection and prioritize Non-Negotiables, demonstrating integrity and accountability.

3. **Unity in Diversity:** The challenges underscored the importance of Others-Focus, enabling leaders to respond with empathy, collaboration, and acceptance even in the face of internal division.

Reflective Questions:

1. **Guiding Honor:** Consider a situation where you had to make a tough decision that balanced short-term benefits with long-term values. How could a commitment to high Honor guide your choices in such scenarios?

2. **Prioritizing Others:** Reflect on an experience of collaboration during adversity. How did prioritizing Others-Focus contribute to a positive resolution?

Compelling Action Steps:

1. **Cultivate Honorable Decision-Making:** When faced with dilemmas, engage in Reflection to evaluate options in alignment with Non-Negotiables. Prioritize the long-term impact on stakeholders over short-term gains.

The journey of the leaders of Danalgo through challenges and setbacks reinforces the transformative power of high Honor. Adversity tests the authenticity of their commitment and underscores their growth. Their responses to challenges serve as a testament to the integration of the HONOR Code as a guiding force in their leadership journey. Their ability to uphold ethical principles amid adversity reaffirms that the transformation they embarked upon is a personal endeavor and a foundational shift that shapes their actions and the destiny of their organization. The path of resilience they tread illuminates the capacity of Honor-driven leadership to prevail over adversity and inspire positive change in leadership, families, and culture.

Chapter 8: The Final Test

Trial by Fire

In the heart of Danalgo, a pivotal moment unfolded—one that would put the leaders' Honor to the ultimate test. The organization faced a significant crisis, one that threatened its reputation and the safety and trust of its customers. A faulty product caused a series of unfortunate events, raising concerns about the organization's practices and values.

The crisis prompted an emergency meeting of the leadership team, including Jake McLeash, Maddy Davidson, and other key members. The atmosphere was tense as they gathered to confront the harsh reality of the situation. The stakes were high, and the challenge was daunting. The crisis had the potential to unravel all the progress they made in their journey of transformation.

As the leaders deliberated, the principles of the HONOR Code became their guiding light. Habits cultivated through the Code's pillars provided a foundation of trust and collaboration among the team. Offerings to the community and stakeholders fueled their determination to address the crisis transparently and responsibly. Non-Negotiables formed a shield against compromise, reminding them that upholding truth, integrity, and empathy was paramount. Others-Focus compelled them to consider the impact of their decisions on all those affected, from employees to customers and beyond. Reflection allowed them to pause, reflect on their values, and make decisions rooted in Honorable principles.

The crisis wasn't just a test of their leadership; it was a test of their character. The transformed leaders recognized that their response to this situation would define the organization's future and the legacy they were building. They understood that true leadership wasn't just about success—it was about how they navigated challenges with integrity and Honor.

The crisis cast a spotlight on the core values and principles that had become the heart of Danalgo's transformation. The journey of the leaders was put to the ultimate test, and the world awaited their response.

The outcome of their actions in the face of crisis will reveal their growth and the impact of the HONOR Code on their leadership, families, and culture.

United in Crisis

As the crisis unfolded within Danalgo, the leaders faced a moment that required them to demonstrate their commitment to the HONOR Code in its entirety. The values that had become their guiding principles were put to the test as they grappled with the gravity of the situation.

In response, the leaders exhibited a remarkable display of collaboration, driven by their shared commitment to Honor. Rather than succumbing to panic or individual interests, they convened to develop a comprehensive action plan. Maddy Davidson, their guide in this journey, facilitated an open dialogue that encouraged every voice to be heard.

Their communication was marked by transparency. They acknowledged the severity of the crisis to employees, customers, and stakeholders, providing clear and honest updates on the unfolding events. Their transparent approach maintained trust and demonstrated the authenticity of their Honor, even in the face of adversity.

The decisions they made during this crisis were not influenced by expediency but rooted in their core values. They prioritized the safety and well-being of their customers above all else, reflecting the essence of Others-Focus. They also upheld Non-Negotiables, ensuring that accountability and Honorable conduct remained at the forefront of their actions.

Reflection played a crucial role as they navigated the crisis. Regular moments of introspection allowed them to align their decisions with the principles of the HONOR Code. They acknowledged their own shortcomings, learned from their mistakes, and grew stronger as a result.

In showcasing their collaborative efforts, transparent communication, and decisions grounded in core values, the leaders of Danalgo exemplified the transformational power of the HONOR Code. The crisis became an opportunity to test their commitment and to amplify their positive impact on the organization and its stakeholders.

The story of their collective journey will reveal the magnitude of their transformation and the impact it had on leadership, families, and culture.

Rising from the Ashes

Amidst the trials and tribulations, the leaders of Danalgo showcased remarkable resilience. The crisis that tested their commitment to the HONOR Code became a crucible for their growth and transformation. As the storm began to subside, the organization emerged stronger, more united, and firmly anchored in the principles of Honor.

Their transparent and collaborative efforts preserved trust and forged deeper connections among the leadership team. The sense of unity that developed during the crisis carried over into their everyday interactions, fostering a culture of support, mutual respect, and shared purpose.

The positive outcomes of their high Honor approach were evident throughout the organization. Employee engagement reached unprecedented levels as team members felt empowered by the transparency and commitment to core values. Stakeholders recognized the genuine dedication to their well-being, strengthening Danalgo's reputation in the industry.

Amid the crisis, as news of the faulty product emerged, the leaders of Danalgo were faced with a defining moment that showcased their Others-Focus. Recognizing the potential impact on customers' safety, they swiftly initiated a multi-faceted response that spoke volumes about their dedication to the community they served.

First, a cross-functional team was assembled, composed of experts from various departments within the organization. Their collective goal was to address the crisis comprehensively and transparently. This team conducted a thorough analysis of the issue, identifying the root cause of the problem and potential risks to customers. This transparency and accountability formed the backbone of their strategy.

Simultaneously, the organization launched an immediate recall of the faulty products, putting customer safety above all else. The recall process was not merely about retrieving defective products; it was also about safeguarding the trust that customers had placed in the organization. Each step was carefully designed to ensure that affected customers felt heard, understood, and supported.

In addition to the recall, the leaders of Danalgo took proactive steps to rectify the situation for affected customers. They provided clear and accessible channels for customers to report any issues or concerns. A dedicated customer support team was established to assist those who needed assistance or information. Compensation and solutions were offered to affected customers, not as a legal obligation, but as a genuine gesture of care and responsibility.

Beyond their immediate customer base, the leaders extended their commitment to community and service to suppliers and partners who were also impacted by the crisis. They engaged in open dialogues with suppliers, explaining the situation transparently and working collaboratively to mitigate the fallout. The focus was not just on the financial implications but also on maintaining strong relationships based on trust and mutual understanding.

Perhaps most impactful was their response to the crisis's broader implications. The leaders channeled their resources to support initiatives that aimed to prevent similar incidents industry-wide. They invested in research and development, ensuring that the lessons learned from the crisis would contribute to advancements in product safety and quality standards.

Throughout this process, their Others-Focus was evident in every action taken. They went above and beyond legal requirements to ensure the safety and well-being of their customers and stakeholders. Their decision-making was guided by empathy and a sincere desire to make amends. By putting the interests of others before their own, they salvaged trust and strengthened the bonds of community that underpinned their organization.

In retrospect, the crisis served as an unexpected platform for the leaders to demonstrate their wholehearted dedication to the principles of the HONOR Code. Their actions during this challenging time were not driven by publicity or reputation management but by an authentic desire to serve and uplift. Through their responses, they embodied the essence of transformational leadership that places others at the center—a living testament to the transformative power of the HONOR Code in action.

In the wake of the storm, the organization found itself on a new trajectory—one guided by principles that transformed their leadership and their entire culture. The high Honor approach had become more than a code—it was now woven into the fabric of Danalgo's identity.

We're going to explore Honor from a scientific perspective. A neuroscience symposium will open doors to understanding how the principles of the HONOR Code resonate with the human brain and illuminate the path to lasting transformation.

Reflections 3-2-1

The crucible of crisis tested their leadership acumen and the essence of their character. As we go deeper into this chapter, we unravel a tale of resilience, integrity, and unwavering commitment to the principles of the HONOR Code.

Lessons Learned: In this chapter, we embarked on a journey through the fire of crisis, witnessing the leaders of Danalgo confront adversity head-on. We learned that even in the face of the most daunting challenges, the transformation fueled by the HONOR Code can be a beacon of hope. Their response to the crisis was a testament to the power of collaboration, transparency, and strong core values.

Key Takeaways:

1. **Unity Amidst Crisis:** The crisis underscored the strength of collaboration. The leaders united, combining their diverse strengths to develop a comprehensive action plan highlighting the significance of a cohesive team that is guided by shared values.

2. **Transparency Sustains Trust:** Transparent communication was the linchpin that held the organization together during turbulent times. The

leaders' openness about the situation, challenges, and progress upheld the trust of employees, customers, and stakeholders alike.

3. **Values as True North:** When faced with the crisis, the leaders leaned on their core values to navigate treacherous waters. The HONOR Code's principles of Non-Negotiables and Others-Focus guided their decisions, ensuring that their response was not just tactical but also ethically sound.

Reflective Questions:

1. **Transparent Communication:** In what ways did transparency impact the outcomes of the crisis for Danalgo? How can transparent communication be integrated into our own leadership practices, especially during difficult times?

2. **Core Values:** Reflect on a personal experience where you faced a challenge that tested your commitment to your core values. How did you navigate the situation, and what were the outcomes?

Compelling Action Steps:

1. **Amplify Collaboration:** Strive to create a collaborative environment within your team or organization. Embrace diverse perspectives, encourage open dialogue, and foster a sense of unity that transcends challenges.

As we emerge from the flames of crisis alongside the leaders of Danalgo, we see a change to a higher standard of leadership. Their actions during the crisis revealed the depth of their growth and the impact of the HONOR Code on leadership, families, and culture.

Chapter 9: The Neuroscience of Honor
Unveiling the Mind's Tapestry

A new chapter dawned at Danalgo, one that transcended the boundaries of the organization and went into the realms of science and the human mind. The concept of Honor, as embodied in the HONOR Code, ignited a spark of curiosity that led to the organization hosting a groundbreaking event—a neuroscience symposium dedicated to exploring the intricate connection between Honor and the human brain.

The symposium gathered esteemed experts from various fields—neuroscientists, psychologists, ethicists, and leaders who had embraced the HONOR Code. These individuals came together with a shared goal: to uncover the neural underpinnings of Honorable behavior and understand how the principles of Honor could reshape the way we perceive leadership, families, and culture.

As participants filed into the symposium venue, a sense of anticipation hung in the air. The stage was set for a captivating journey through the mysteries of the mind and the transformative potential of Honor. Attendees from different walks of life exchanged eager glances, united by their shared belief in the power of positive change.

Maddy Davidson, who played a pivotal role in leading the transformation at Danalgo, stood at the podium to welcome the attendees. Her presence exemplified the embodiment of the HONOR Code, and her words resonated with the essence of the journey that brought them all together.

"In embracing the HONOR Code, we embarked on a journey of self-discovery, transformation, and impact," Maddy began. "Today, we gather to celebrate the progress we've made and to explore the very science that underscores the transformative power of Honor."

With those words, the symposium commenced—an exploration that would uncover the neural intricacies of Honorable behavior and the potential for neuroplasticity. The speakers who followed would unravel the ways in which the brain responded to acts of Honor, compassion, and Honorable decision-making, painting a vivid picture of how these principles could reshape individuals, organizations, and societies.

As the symposium unfolded, the attendees found themselves immersed in a dialogue that bridged the gap between the science of the brain and the art of leading with Honor. The journey of Jake McLeash, Maddy Davidson, and the leaders of Danalgo ignited a larger movement—one that extended far beyond their organization's walls and ventured into the very fabric of humanity's potential for positive transformation.

We'll dive deeper into the symposium's discussions and explore the neural mechanisms that underlie Honorable behavior, as well as the exciting potential for neuroplasticity. The revelations that awaited would shed light on the impact of Honor on the way we think, act, and lead.

Exploring the Neuroscience Honorable Behaviors

The symposium's agenda was rich with insightful presentations, panel discussions, and workshops that explored the intricate dance between the brain's neural circuitry and the practice of Honor. Experts from diverse fields united to shed light on the mechanisms underlying Honorable behavior and the potential for neuroplasticity—the brain's remarkable ability to rewire itself in response to experiences and intentional practices.

Neuroscientists presented cutting-edge research that highlighted how specific regions of the brain were activated when individuals engaged in acts of Honor and compassion. The discussions wove a captivating narrative, revealing how empathy, gratitude, and moral decision-making had tangible neural correlates. Attendees were captivated as they learned how the brain responded to acts of kindness and integrity, substantiating the notion that Honor was not just an abstract concept but a tangible force shaping our neural pathways.

The Spark of Neuroplasticity

The concept of neuroplasticity drew a bridge between science and the transformations that occurred within Danalgo. As presenters discussed the brain's ability to adapt and rewire itself based on intentional practices, the audience was reminded of Jake's journey from a traditional CEO to an advocate for the HONOR Code. His experiences, his evolution, and his leadership transformation were now seen through the lens of scientific possibility—neuroplasticity offering a framework that validated the changes he had undergone.

Maddy Davidson took the stage once more. "Neuroplasticity teaches us that we are not bound by our old ways of thinking and behaving. Our brains are malleable, capable of change and growth. This understanding empowers us to forge a path of Honor, not just as a philosophical choice, but as a transformational journey at a neurological level."

As the symposium's sessions continued, the participants engaged in thought-provoking dialogues about the interplay between science, ethics, and leadership. The insights gained were intellectually stimulating and deeply personal, igniting a renewed sense of purpose and commitment among the leaders.

The symposium's scientific revelations ignite a renewed passion within Jake McLeash, Maddy Davidson, and their fellow leaders..

Connecting Honor and Neuroscience

The symposium was a blend of inspiration and enlightenment, forging a powerful link between the principles of the HONOR Code and the scientific intricacies of the brain. As the discussions unfolded and the experts illuminated the neural pathways of Honorable behavior, the leaders in attendance found themselves drawn into an exploration of their journey toward increased Honor.

Jake McLeash sat in rapt attention, his mind weaving together the threads of his personal transformation with the scientific insights being shared. The symposium validated his choices, the shifts in his habits, the deeper connection he established with his colleagues and community, and the unwavering Honorable leadership. As he listened, Jake could not help but reflect on his own path, a path that shaped him and catalyzed a movement within Danalgo.

Maddy Davidson stood at the intersection of science and leadership philosophy, the HONOR Code was not merely a set of abstract principles—it was a roadmap to rewiring the brain for integrity, compassion, and collaboration. The symposium revealed the scientific underpinnings of their journey, reinforcing her conviction that transformation was not a one-time event but a continuous process of growth and renewal.

A New Depth to the Journey of Honor

The symposium's impact extended beyond the event itself. The leaders emerged with a newfound understanding—a conviction that their pursuit of Honor was the right path and scientifically validated. Armed with the knowledge of neuroplasticity and Honorable neural pathways, they felt a deeper sense of responsibility to cultivate their own minds and those of their teams.

Maddy Davidson addressed the gathering with a sense of urgency and determination. "As we leave this symposium, let us remember that our Honor is not just a lofty ideal. It's a transformative force that reshapes our brains, influences our actions, and reverberates through our organizations and communities. Armed with this knowledge, we can lead with even greater purpose, knowing that our journey towards Honor is backed by science."

Reflections 3-2-1

In the radiant illumination of the neuroscience symposium, the leaders of Danalgo discovered the union of science and Honor, uncovering the intricate tapestry that binds the principles of the HONOR Code with the human brain. This chapter has enriched our understanding of how Honor intertwines with neural pathways, and how it reshapes leadership and the essence of our being.

Lessons Learned: This chapter has transported us from the heart of Danalgo's transformation to the realm of neuroscience, forging a bridge between abstract principles and neural realities. We learned that Honor, once perceived as a subjective concept, can be traced within the very fibers of our brain, manifesting in acts of kindness, empathy, and Honorable decision-making.

Key Takeaways:

1. **The Neural Dance of Honor:** The symposium revealed the neural signatures of Honorable behavior. Specific brain regions were illuminated as they fired during acts of compassion and moral choice. This unveils the tangible nature of Honor—a force that orchestrates the brain's response to integrity and empathy.

2. **Neuroplasticity: The Brain's Symphony of Change:** Neuroplasticity, the brain's ability to rewire itself, resonates harmoniously with the journey of transformation undertaken by the leaders. This concept validates the changes in habits, perspectives, and values that result from embracing the HONOR Code.

3. **Science as the Catalyst of Purpose:** The symposium fused science and philosophy, kindling a renewed sense of purpose among the leaders. Their journey toward Honor has now been fortified with the knowledge that their commitment has scientific roots, lending even greater urgency to their mission.

Reflective Questions:

1. **Honorable behavior:** How does the intersection of neuroscience and Honor alter your perception of leadership and personal growth? Reflect on instances where you've witnessed the tangible effects of Honorable behavior in yourself and others.

2. **Honorable habits:** Consider the concept of neuroplasticity. How can the knowledge that our brains are adaptable inspire us to consciously cultivate Honorable habits and behaviors?

Compelling Action Steps:

1. **Embrace Informed Leadership:** Integrate the insights from the symposium into your leadership philosophy. Recognize that your commitment to Honor aligns with ethics and the scientific potential of the brain's neural plasticity.

As we emerge from the symposium, a symphony of science and Honor, we stand at the cusp of a new understanding. The nexus between the HONOR Code and neuroscience has unlocked insights into the transformative power of embracing Honor. The leaders of Danalgo have discovered that their journey of growth and transformation is not merely a subjective pursuit—it's a journey aligned with the very architecture of the brain.

The transformative journey initiated by the HONOR Code has the potential to change individual lives and entire communities and cultures. We are poised to witness the culmination of their journey and the legacy they are leaving behind.

Chapter 10: Insights from Neuroscience

A Revelation of Honor's Roots

The symposium had been a gathering of minds—a convergence of science and philosophy, of leadership and neuroscience. As the leaders absorbed the revelations shared within its walls, they discovered an intricate tapestry that wove together the principles of the HONOR Code with the inner workings of the human brain.

Where Science Meets Values

Jake McLeash stood before his peers, his gaze reflecting a newfound depth of understanding. The revelations from the symposium affirmed his commitment to the HONOR Code principles, unveiling the alignment between his values and the neural mechanisms that underpin Honorable behavior. "It's remarkable," he mused, "how science and Honor converge to create positive change. Our journey has not only transformed us—it has been validated by the very fabric of our minds."

Maddy Davidson dedicated her life to helping leaders embrace Honor, and the symposium magnified her impact. "These insights bridge the gap between theory and practice," she shared. "The symposium has shown us that our pursuit of Honor shapes our thoughts, actions, and the very essence of who we are."

An Unbreakable Bond

The revelations were a testament to the power of the HONOR Code. They unearthed a neural foundation for the principles that Jake, Maddy, and their fellow leaders championed. The symposium illuminated the neuroscience behind their journey, reinforcing their commitment to leading with Honor, empathy, and authenticity.

The leaders left the symposium with a heightened sense of purpose—a deepened resolve to uphold the HONOR Code in every aspect of their lives. They were armed with values and the understanding of how those values were etched into the neural pathways of their minds.

The practical applications of cognitive load theory, mirror neurons, and emotional engagement give us insights to further understand and internalize Honor, providing leaders with the tools to navigate the complex landscape of leadership with clarity, empathy, and unyielding integrity.

Cognitive Load Theory: This theory illuminates the intricate relationship between our cognitive resources and the demands of tasks we undertake. When applied to Honor, it unveils the significance of mental clarity in ethical decision-making. By consciously managing cognitive load, leaders can ensure that their minds are unburdened by unnecessary distractions, enabling them to focus on ethical considerations and make decisions rooted in integrity. This concept empowers leaders to simplify complexities, prioritize ethical values, and navigate dilemmas with a clear conscience.

Mirror Neurons: At the core of human empathy lies mirror neurons—a neurological phenomenon that enables us to emotionally resonate with another's experience. By understanding and harnessing mirror neurons, leaders can foster a deep sense of empathy within themselves and their teams. This empathy enables them to genuinely understand others' perspectives, feel their emotions, and respond with kindness and consideration. By consciously activating mirror neurons, leaders can build strong relationships, bridge communication gaps, and create an HONOR culture of trust and respect.

Emotional Engagement: Emotions are a powerful driving force behind human behavior. Emotional engagement, when channeled in alignment with Honor, empowers leaders to make decisions that prioritize the well-being of all stakeholders. Leaders who engage emotionally with their teams and stakeholders are more likely to recognize the impact of their decisions on others' lives. This heightened emotional awareness compels them to make choices that serve the organization's interests and uphold their ethical commitments. Emotional engagement thus acts as a compass guiding leaders to navigate the complex landscape of leadership with authenticity and compassion.

In unison, these concepts provide a framework for living an honorable life. Cognitive load theory ensures that the mind is clear and receptive to Honorable considerations, enabling leaders to make principled decisions. Mirror neurons infuse interactions with empathy, fostering meaningful connections and Honorable behavior. Emotional engagement aligns leaders' decisions with the well-being of all, enriching the Honor in their actions.

By integrating these concepts, leaders are equipped with invaluable tools to uphold the principles of the HONOR Code even in the face of challenges. In a world where leadership can be intricate and demanding, these insights offer a guide to navigate with clarity, integrity, and a deep sense of humanity. As leaders strive to cultivate Honorable behavior, these concepts offer a roadmap to transform their intentions into tangible, Honorable actions that shape their own lives and the lives of those they influence.

With each insight, the leaders recognized the significance of their journey. They saw how cognitive load theory emphasized the importance of simplifying communication and decision-making processes, allowing core values to shine through. The concept of mirror neurons resonated as a reminder that their actions and behaviors were contagious, influencing others in profound ways.

Emotional engagement, the cornerstone of building connections and fostering empathy, became a key discovery in their pursuit of Honor. The leaders understood that creating an environment where individuals felt seen and heard was not just a matter of courtesy, but a cognitive and emotional strategy that would uplift their entire organization.

The neuroscience symposium was a turning point. It was a moment of clarity where science met purpose, where understanding met action. The leaders left the symposium armed with knowledge that invigorated their dedication to The HONOR Code. As they returned to their roles, the principles of HONOR became more than just words; they were deeply ingrained in their consciousness, influencing every decision and interaction. This newfound understanding was about to guide them through a new phase of their transformative journey.

Reflections 3-2-1

In this chapter, we uncovered the intricate relationship between neuroscience and the HONOR Code. The symposium revealed the neural pathways that underlie honorable behavior. This convergence of insights impacted our understanding of leadership, relationships, and personal growth.

Lessons Learned: Our exploration into the symposium's revelations unveiled the neural foundations of the HONOR Code principles, affirming that science and ethics are intertwined. Through cognitive load theory, mirror neurons, and emotional engagement, we uncovered the mechanisms that allow Honor to take root within us, reshaping our thoughts and actions.

Key Takeaways:

1. **Unity of Science and Values:** The symposium demonstrated the unbreakable bond between scientific discoveries and our core values. As the symphony of neuroscience and Honor played out, we realized that the pursuit of Honorable leadership is not just a philosophical endeavor; it's a neurologically supported pathway to positive change.

2. **Neuroscience of Connection:** The concept of mirror neurons revealed that empathy is more than a sentiment—it's a neurological phenomenon. By embracing mirror neurons, we open the door to genuine understanding, bridging gaps between individuals and fostering connections that are founded on empathy and compassion.

3. **The Power of Emotional Engagement:** Emotional engagement emerged as a potent force in Honorable leadership. Understanding the impact of emotions on decision-making showed us that our choices extend beyond mere logic. Emotional engagement equips us with a compass to navigate the complexities of leadership while honoring the well-being of all stakeholders.

Reflective Questions:

1. **Ethical Decisions:** How can you apply the insights from cognitive load theory to streamline your decision-making process and ensure ethical considerations take precedence?

2. **Empathetic Interactions:** Reflect on instances where you could harness mirror neurons to enhance your understanding of others' perspectives and foster more empathetic interactions.

Compelling Action Steps:

1. **Cultivate Cognitive Clarity:** Embrace cognitive load theory by decluttering your mind. Prioritize Honorable values by simplifying your decision-making process and focusing on the core principles that guide your actions.

As we move forward, armed with the insights gained from the neuroscience symposium, let us navigate the complexities of leadership with newfound clarity, empathy, and a commitment to the HONOR Code. With each decision and interaction, we have the opportunity to shape a world where ethical leadership is not just a choice but a way of being—a transformation that transcends boundaries and touches lives.

Chapter 11: Silent H- The Power of Habits

The symphony of insights and revelations reached a crescendo, echoing through the halls of understanding and transformation. Jake McLeash found his path ahead was both illuminated and mysterious. His past endeavors and his future aspirations were all wrapped in the cloak of the HONOR Code.

As he gazed out the window, he felt an itch, something vital was missing from the big picture. The symposium revealed the intricate connection between neuroscience and Honor. Yet, there was a silence amidst the crescendo, a silent 'H' was waiting to be heard.

With a sense of urgency, Jake called Maddy. As the line connected, his voice carried curiosity and anticipation. "Maddy, amidst all these insights and revelations, I can't help but feel that something is missing. There's a gap that I can't quite put my finger on."

Maddy's calm voice carried the weight of wisdom and experience. "Jake, my friend, every Honor Champion reaches this point in their journey. It's a moment when the road traveled becomes a crossroads. It's a sign that you're ready for the next phase."

Jake's mind churned. "But what is this next phase, Maddy? What's missing in all of this?"

Maddy reassured him. "Jake, it's the process—the transformation that takes time, the growth that happens in the background. You see, the first pillar of the HONOR Code, the "H" is for Habits. It's where Honor takes root and blooms over time."

Jake's thoughts swirled. "Habits... Of course, it makes sense. The symposium has revealed the 'why' behind Honor. But the 'how,' the practical steps, the daily choices that become our second nature—that's the missing piece."

Maddy continued. "Exactly, Jake. Honor isn't just about understanding principles; it's about embodying them in every action, every decision. It's about the little choices that accumulate over time, augmenting integrity and authenticity."

Jake took a deep breath, "So, what do I do now, Maddy? How do I bridge this gap?"

Maddy guided. "It's your time now, Jake. Time to memorialize your progress, to define the habits that will be the threads woven into your journey. Each thread represents a choice, a commitment to Honor."

Jake nodded with purpose. "I want to capture this phase, Maddy. I want to define the habits that will be the backbone of our journey."

Maddy encouraged him, "You have the wisdom within you, Jake. Trust yourself to define these habits. Write them down, reflect on each one, and let them become your guiding lights."

As the call ended, Jake's mind was ablaze with the path ahead. He would define the habits, the silent 'H' that would solidify the ground beneath every step. In the quiet hours of the night, he began his introspective journey into a future brimming with purpose and Honor.

With the first pillar of the HONOR Code, Habits, as his guide, Jake set out to craft the foundation of his journey towards a more honorable existence.

"Compassion and Empathy"

Jake whispered, the words sinking in, and closed his eyes. Compassion—the bridge between hearts. Empathy—the door to another's world.

With the resolve of an artist envisioning his masterpiece, Jake began crafting the first habit:

Habit 1: Practice Active Listening In the quietude of the night, thoughts unfurled. "Engage in attentive listening when interacting with others, showing genuine interest in their thoughts and feelings." Neurons fired with understanding. Active listening—more than hearing words, it meant truly grasping the speaker's intent. Dopamine surged, an applause of neural recognition, every time he genuinely paid attention.

Habit 2: Put Yourself in Their Shoes Moving to the second stroke, he took a deep breath. "Before judgments, imagine how others feel." Cognitive pathways connected perspectives. It was a neural handshake, empathy's cornerstone. The anterior insula, the emotional compass, recognized stepping into others' shoes.

Habit 3: Offer Support and Encouragement The final stroke beckoned. "Reach out to individuals facing challenges, offer comfort, encouragement, assistance." Brain pathways pulsed. Support activated reward centers in him and those he helped. Oxytocin surged, bonding molecules resonated. By uplifting others, he uplifted himself.

These habits were values in action. Armor against misunderstandings, a shield against disconnection. Anchors in storms, reminding of shared humanity.

"Truthfulness and Integrity,"

These words reverberating in his mind. Truth—the bedrock of trust. Integrity—the compass steering him through all trials.

With the weight of these virtues, Jake kept shaping the habits that would define his honorable path:

Habit 1: Speak Honestly and Transparently Ink flowed, forming the first strokes of his intent. "Communicate openly and truthfully in all conversations. Avoid misleading statements or half-truths." Neural pathways lit up like constellations. Honesty wasn't just words; it was neural harmony, aligning thoughts and speech. Prefrontal cortex hummed, rationality and judgment in symphony.

Habit 2: Admit Mistakes and Take Responsibility Moving on, apprehension mixed with determination. "Acknowledge mistakes honestly, rectify without shifting blame." Neurons fired sparks of realization. Admitting mistakes demanded vulnerability, exposing imperfections. The anterior cingulate cortex recognized courage. Emotional detox, soul cleansing through accountability.

Habit 3: Keep Promises and Commitments Each pen stroke pulsed purpose. "Follow through on commitments, demonstrate reliability." Neural pathways wove determination. Keeping promises was commitment to values, a declaration of dependability. Basal ganglia recognized, etching integrity's neural pathways.

Jake paused, heart stirred by the power of these habits. Truthfulness and integrity were a moral compass. These habits illuminated storms, anchoring him to values.

"Service and Selflessness"

Words resonated within him. Service—a commitment to others. Selflessness—a journey to his core.

With purpose, Jake began to craft the habits of service and selflessness:

Habit 1: Practice Random Acts of Kindness

Pen traced aspirations. "Regularly perform small acts of kindness without expecting return." Words formed, heart expanding. Kindness—a deliberate action, joy radiating. The brain's reward centers acknowledged the intrinsic happiness in selfless giving.

Habit 2: Volunteer Time and Skills

Each pen stroke linked Jake to the world. "Volunteer for community service, utilize skills." Neurons hummed in unity. Volunteering—an investment in well-being, unity's power. The brain's striatum pulsed, empathy and action in symphony.

Habit 3: Offer Help Even When Inconvenient

Turning to the third habit, determination deepened. "Help others even when it sacrifices time or convenience." Words echoed in his chest. Selflessness—a choice demanding courage. Emotional conductor, anterior cingulate cortex, stirred. This habit tuned neural pathways to empathy and sacrifice's frequency.

Jake absorbed these habits' significance. Service and selflessness—embodiments of humanity's connection. Not just actions; declarations of commitment to greater good, belief in compassion's power.

"Respect for All"

Jake murmured, words settling in. Respect—a heart's bridge. All—every voice mattered.

Renewed, he shaped habits of respect:

Habit 1: Listen Without Judgment Pen moved, ink trails etched. "Open conversations, no judging perspectives." Writing freed him, unlocking understanding. The brain's ventromedial prefrontal cortex acknowledged a mind without prejudice.

Habit 2: Acknowledge and Validate Others Empathy surged with the next habit. "Recognize others' contributions, value their input." Pen on paper, unity's canvas. Validation—not just a nod, but an affirmation of shared humanity. The brain's insula sensed empathy's emotions.

Habit 3: Include Everyone Echoes of resonance as he reached the last. "Mindful choices, respect all regardless of background." Words are an anthem of unity. Inclusion—a warm embrace beyond differences. The brain's anterior cingulate cortex hummed approval, harmonizing neural pathways to acceptance's tune.

Jake paused, heart full. Respect for all—a way of being. Not just principles—embodied commitment to a world where every voice, perspective, and individual mattered.

"Forgiveness and Reconciliation"

Jake whispered, words heavy with meaning. Forgiveness—a healing balm. Reconciliation—a bridge to mend.

Pen poised, habits took shape:

Habit 1: Practice Letting Go Eyes closed, memories navigated. "Reflect, release resentment." Steps to emotional freedom. Let go—reclaiming space. The brain's anterior cingulate cortex recognized the therapeutic release.

Habit 2: Initiate Conversations Determination ignited. "Address conflicts proactively." Words surged with courage. Initiate—not waiting but leading. The brain's dorsolateral prefrontal cortex recognized strength in proactive resolve.

Habit 3: Seek Common Ground Unity's promise stirred him. "Find shared understanding." Pen danced, building bridges. Seek— connections beyond differences. The brain's prefrontal cortex resonated, eager for shared understanding.

Jake leaned back, eyes on the page. Forgiveness and reconciliation—beyond conflict, reclaiming well-being and unity. More than habits—a declaration to heal and unite.

"Humility"

Jake whispered, reverence in the air. Humility—the quiet strength. Gratitude, vulnerability, celebrating others—the essence of a true leader. Pen moved, capturing humility's core:

Habit 1: Express Gratitude Eyes closed, words sinking. "Express appreciation, acknowledge others." Gratitude—heartfelt tapestry of support. The brain's anterior cingulate cortex warmed to acknowledging others' efforts.

Habit 2: Admit When You Don't Know Vulnerability's touch. "Admit lack of knowledge, seek wisdom." Admit—embracing humility. The brain's dorsolateral prefrontal cortex accepted diverse knowledge sources.

Habit 3: Celebrate Others' Achievements Humility that elevates. "Celebrate without jealousy." Celebration—shared victories. The brain's ventral striatum lit up with shared joy.

Jake leaned back, notebook in hand, fulfilled. Humility wasn't just a posture; it was leadership's essence. Not habits—testament to leadership as connection, not domination.

He smiled, journey in mind. Humility wasn't insignificance; it was wisdom. Not surrendering power; embracing strength. Leadership—connecting with everyone's greatness, including his own.

"GRACE© and Conflict Resolution"

Jake pondered words bridging complexities and habits. Not resolving conflicts but touching them with GRACE.

Habit 1: Practice Deep Breathing Imagine storms, emotions. "Deep breathing, anchor in emotions." The brain's amygdala softened, deep breath taming waves.

Habit 2: Use GRACE Pen with reverence, his path's light. "Use GRACE: Gentle tone, Raw facts, Share assumptions, Check assumptions, Explore solutions." GRACE—not an acronym but a conflict compass. The brain's anterior cingulate cortex resonated, recognizing harmony in GRACE.

Habit 3: Find Common Solutions Unity, diversity's harmony. "Collaborate for shared solutions." Collaboration—a tapestry of shared understanding. Brain's prefrontal cortex affirmed, solutions for all.

Jake leaned back, wisdom in hand. GRACE—transforming conflict into conversation. Habits weren't tools; they were leading with GRACE, turning conflicts into opportunities.

He smiled, habits building bridges. GRACE—a philosophy, not just technique. Conflicts—narratives to rewrite.

"Honorable Decision-Making"

Jake whispered, heart resonating with weighty words. Decisions—leadership's cornerstone, shaping paths. Yet, true leaders aren't defined just by choices, but the thought behind them.

Habit 1: Reflect Before Acting He wrote, feeling responsibility's gravity. "Reflect on ethical implications before deciding." Beyond impact, it's about tracing ripples. The brain's dorsolateral prefrontal cortex affirmed, thoughtful contemplation's value.

Habit 2: Consult Trusted Advisors Pause, mentors' wisdom remembered. "Seek guidance from trusted mentors for ethical dilemmas." Advisors—more than information, they're fog-piercing beacons. The brain's anterior cingulate cortex recognized wisdom's search.

Habit 3: Consider Long-Term Consequences Pen's movement, foresight's tendrils. "Evaluate decisions' lasting impact on well-being, relationships." Long-term—seeds for a wisdom-nurtured future. The brain's prefrontal cortex embraced destiny's shaping.

Reviewing, Jake saw ethical leadership's essence. Power wields choices, but responsibility wields ethics. Outcomes echo intentions—ripples shaping legacies.

"Unconditional Love"

Jake pondered, words vibrating with purpose. Love—a transformative force shaping lives, bonds, and healing. In leadership's vast reach, this force unlocked connections beyond barriers.

Habit 1: Practice Kindness to Strangers He penned, empathy's threads entwining. "Extend kindness to daily encounters with strangers." Kindness—humanity's offering, not confined to circles. The brain's mirror neurons resonated, understanding outreach's beauty.

Habit 2: Offer Support During Tough Times Reflection on impactful support. "Reach out to offer solace during tough times." Support—a haven in storms, beyond solving. The brain's anterior cingulate cortex acknowledged solace's value.

Habit 3: Forgive Without Conditions Weighty words, humbling and freeing. "Forgive, embodying unconditional grace and love." Forgiveness—embracing imperfections. Brain's hippocampus recognized healing's release.

Through habits, Unconditional Love emerged—a choice beyond differences, a balm for flaws. These weren't just about love; they were about mending, uplifting, uniting.

Love meant more than emotion—it was a responsibility, nurturing bonds, bridging gaps. Notebook closed, warmth affirmed: leadership meant connection. Habits weren't just about leading; they were about boundless, condition-less loving—connecting beyond measure.

"Courage to Stand for Truth"

Jake deliberated, determination surging. Truth—the bedrock of integrity, guiding honorable actions. He etched habits embodying unwavering commitment:

Habit 1: Speak Up for Injustice Weighted words—confronting wrongs head-on. "Courageously address injustice and advocate for what's right." Speaking up—more than voicing; it was truth's beacon in adversity. Brain's dorsolateral prefrontal cortex aligned with upholding justice.

Habit 2: Advocate for Vulnerable Populations Conviction magnified with each word. "Raise voice for marginalized, support the vulnerable." Advocacy—beyond sympathy, an influencer for a better world. The brain's anterior cingulate cortex echoed amplifying voices.

Habit 3: Be a Truth-Seeker Reflection—truth as growth catalyst. "Seek truth, embrace discomfort in challenging beliefs." Truth-seeking—unmasking falsehoods, nurturing curiosity. Brain's hippocampus embraced continuous growth.

These habits—Courage to Stand for Truth—not just confronting injustices, but internal barriers. Not just demanding truth from world, demanding truth from oneself.

Truth wasn't notion; it was commitment—upholding values against challenge, unpopularity. These habits—asserting truth with courage, anchored in principles.

"Practicing Honorable Leadership"

Jake's whisper carried purpose—a leadership that uplifted, inspired. He crafted habits embodying this responsibility:

Habit 1: Prioritize Team Development Core commitment echoed. "Invest in team's growth and well-being." Prioritizing—more than delegation, active potential cultivation. The brain's anterior cingulate cortex emphasized nurturing leadership's human side.

Habit 2: Lead by Serving Immersed in tasks supporting team's progress. "Take on tasks for their success, showing commitment." Serving—beyond authority, humility in action. Brain's insula highlighted leading through action.

Habit 3: Acknowledge Mistakes Tinge of vulnerability—and strength. "Lead by admitting mistakes, showing authenticity." Acknowledging—beyond flawless authority, fostering growth through authenticity. The brain's prefrontal cortex aligned with embracing mistakes for progress.

Each habit—Practicing Honorable Leadership, embodiment of trust. Not just leadership; guide, mentor, supporter.

Leadership—elevating alongside, not above. Habits—celebrating growth, meeting struggles with empathy, cultivating a culture of elevation.

"Understanding the Bigger Picture"

Jake whispered, heart overflowing with purpose. The pinnacle of clarity—where meaning transcends mundane. He penned habits leading to profound understanding:

Habit 1: Reflect on Core Values Ink flowed—reflection on anchoring values. "Regularly align decisions with higher purpose." Reflecting—beyond assessing, going deep. The brain's hippocampus echoed values' significance.

Habit 2: Seek Spiritual Connection Weight of words—invitation beyond tangible. "Deepen spiritual connection, broaden perspective." Seeking—more than rituals, understanding beyond surface. The brain's default mode network amplified the call for expanded awareness.

Habit 3: Practice Detachment Tracing words—calm, freedom beyond possessions. "Cultivate detachment from material, focus on spiritual growth." Practicing—freedom from chains, finding intangible liberation. The brain's amygdala affirmed true richness in experiences.

Each habit—Understanding the Bigger Picture, journey into depth. Beyond envisioning, embodying essence. These habits—feeling the pulse of existence, embracing eternity.

Understanding the bigger picture—eternal legacy, not in stone but in hearts touched.

Reflections 3-2-1

Lessons Learned: In this chapter, we explored the concept of Habits—the first pillar of the HONOR Code. We learned that while understanding the principles of Honor is crucial, it's the daily habits that truly shape our character and guide our actions.

Key Takeaways:

1. Habits are the foundation of Honor, representing the practical embodiment of its principles in our daily lives.

2. The power of Habits lies in their consistency; small choices accumulate over time to create significant transformations.

3. Crafting intentional Habits requires self-awareness, commitment, and a deep understanding of the values we uphold.

Reflective Questions:

1. **Habits:** What aspects of your life could benefit from the introduction of new Honor-driven habits?

2. **Choices:** Reflect on a moment when your habits influenced a significant outcome. How did your choices shape the result?

Compelling Action Step:

1. Identify one new Honor-based habit you would like to cultivate in the next month and set a plan for its integration.

As Jake closed the chapter on Habits, he found himself standing at the threshold of transformation. The journey ahead was illuminated by the guiding principles of Honor, and the tapestry he weaved would be defined by the threads of intentional habits. With the symphony of insights resonating in his mind, he took the first steps towards crafting a life that echoed the rhythm of Honor—a life where character and action danced harmoniously.

Chapter 12: The Improv Workshop
Yes, And... to Honor

Jake handed his first draft of Danalgo's new Habits of Honor over to his marketing department to be refined. Reflecting their new Honor culture, Jake will assemble a cross functional team to create a second draft of the Habits. They will iterate until they agree on the Habits of Honor the employees of Danalgo will commit to in order to bring their vision into daily practice.

One morning, as he savored his coffee and browsed his emails, a captivating invitation grabbed his attention. It announced an improv comedy workshop—an event aimed at refining communication skills, fostering creativity, and encouraging collaboration. Intrigued and curious, Jake began to consider the potential link between improvisation and the pursuit of Honor.

Driven by his curiosity, he shared the idea with Maddy Davidson, his guide on this journey of embracing The HONOR Code. Maddy listened intently and a knowing smile graced her lips. "Jake, improv entails much more than comedy; it serves as a potent tool for cultivating the qualities aligned with Honor," she gently explained. "Improvisation is about embracing ambiguity, active listening, collaboration, and, notably, adopting the 'Yes, And...' approach."

Jake's curiosity ignited. "Yes, And...?" he echoed, a quizzical expression on his face.

Maddy nodded. "Yes, And... is a core principle of improv. It involves accepting your partner's contribution and building upon it. In the context of our journey, it signifies embracing diverse viewpoints, listening deeply, and collaborating synergistically. It harmonizes beautifully with the Others' Focus pillar of The HONOR Code."

Jake was intrigued. He had always seen himself as a thoughtful and rational leader, but he had to admit that there was room for improvement in his communication and collaboration skills. The idea of an improv workshop suddenly seemed like an exciting opportunity to bridge that gap.

With Maddy's encouragement, Jake shared the idea with his leadership team, and they were surprisingly receptive. Together, they decided to attend the workshop as a group, viewing it as a chance to explore the application of improv tools in their journey toward increased Honor.

As the date of the workshop drew near, Jake found himself both excited and apprehensive. He wondered how improv techniques could truly align with the principles of The HONOR Code. What would he learn, and how would it impact his leadership style? With these questions in mind, Jake McLeash prepared to embark on a new adventure—one that held the potential to transform his leadership and the culture of Danalgo.

Improv and Honor Align

As Jake and his team stepped into the vibrant atmosphere of the improv workshop, they were met with an air of excitement and anticipation. The workshop facilitator, a seasoned improv artist named Maya, welcomed them with a warm smile and a promise of an engaging experience. Maya explained the foundational principle of "Yes, And..."—a cornerstone of improvisational theater.

"Imagine you're on stage with a scene partner," Maya began. "When your partner presents an idea or a situation, the 'Yes, And...' approach encourages you to accept their input ('Yes') and build upon it ('And...'). This fosters a collaborative environment where every idea is valued, and creativity thrives."

Jake could already see the parallels between "Yes, And..." and the Others' Focus pillar of The HONOR Code. The principle emphasized openness, acceptance, and collaboration—the very qualities that Jake was working to cultivate in himself and his organization. It reminded him of the importance of embracing diverse perspectives, which was essential in creating a culture where everyone felt valued and heard.

Maya then introduced the concept of active listening—another skill integral to improv. "Active listening is about fully engaging with your scene partner's words and body language," she explained. "It helps you respond authentically and build a scene together. It's not just about waiting for your turn to speak; it's about truly understanding and connecting."

As the workshop progressed, Jake and his team participated in various improv exercises that required them to practice "Yes, And..." and active listening. Through these activities, they experienced firsthand how a simple shift in mindset could transform their interactions. They found themselves letting go of preconceived notions, embracing spontaneity, and collaborating in ways they hadn't before.

By the end of the workshop, the participants experienced a subtle transformation. They realized that "Yes, And..." and active listening weren't just tools for improv; they were principles that could be seamlessly integrated into their daily interactions. These concepts aligned perfectly with the respectful and collaborative interactions encouraged by The HONOR Code.

As they left the workshop, Jake and his team carried with them a renewed sense of purpose. They saw the potential for these improv principles to enrich their communication, foster creativity, and enhance their Honor. The journey of embracing The HONOR Code was taking them down unexpected paths, and each step brought them closer to a culture that celebrated respect, collaboration, and meaningful connections.

Overcome with Improv

The journey of incorporating improv principles into their organizational culture was far from linear for Jake and his team. Challenges arose as they navigated the complexities of real-world scenarios. The initial enthusiasm wavered as they confronted the realities of change and the resistance that often accompanies it.

One of the significant challenges was helping team members overcome their fear of failure. Improv encourages experimentation and risk-taking, qualities not always associated with a corporate environment. Some team members hesitated to voice their ideas, concerned about the potential for mistakes. Jake recognized that this fear was hindering the open and accepting atmosphere they were striving to create.

However, the breakthroughs were equally remarkable. Jake saw a shift in the team's mindset as they began to appreciate the value of failure as a stepping stone to growth. Through open discussions and sharing personal experiences, team members started to view mistakes as opportunities for learning and innovation.

Another breakthrough came in the form of improved communication. The "Yes, And..." approach led to a noticeable decrease in misunderstandings and conflicts. Team members found that actively listening and building upon each other's ideas led to more effective solutions and strengthened their working relationships.

As time went on, the improv principles became ingrained in their interactions, sparking a culture of collaboration and creativity that extended beyond the boardroom. They embraced the spirit of spontaneity and adaptation, leading to more agile decision-making and innovative problem-solving.

The newfound culture also extended to the development of their organizational offerings. The team approached projects with a fresh perspective, incorporating diverse viewpoints and tapping into the creativity of every individual. The resulting innovations were a testament to the power of collaboration inspired by improv principles.

In their journey to embrace improv, Jake and his team discovered that the challenges were worth the breakthroughs. The principles that they learned from the improv workshop aligned seamlessly with the principles of The HONOR Code, reinforcing the importance of respectful interactions, acceptance, and fostering a culture of growth and innovation.

As the echoes of laughter from the improv workshop faded, a renewed sense of camaraderie settled within the walls of Danalgo. The challenges and breakthroughs they experienced through embracing improv principles began to reshape their interactions, fostering a culture of collaboration and creativity. Energized by their progress, Jake and his team were eager to take the next step—integrating these newfound lessons into their daily interactions. The journey toward aligning improv with The HONOR Code was far from over, but the groundwork had been laid, and the leaders were ready to embrace the transformation ahead.

Reflections 3-2-1

Lessons Learned: In this chapter, we explored the intersection of improvisation and the core principles of The HONOR Code. We discovered that the principles of "Yes, And..." and active listening from improv align seamlessly with the Others' Focus pillar of The HONOR Code, fostering collaboration, acceptance, and respectful interactions.

Key Takeaways:

1. **Alignment of Principles:** The "Yes, And..." approach in improv mirrors the importance of embracing diverse perspectives and fostering collaborative interactions, as emphasized by the Others' Focus pillar of The HONOR Code.

2. **Active Listening as Connection:** The active listening technique practiced in improv resonates with the core value of genuinely understanding and connecting with others, promoting a culture of meaningful communication.

3. **Transformative Potential:** The lessons from the improv workshop revealed that the principles learned aren't just tools for a theatrical stage; they are principles that can reshape organizational interactions and enrich the culture of Honor.

Reflective Questions:

1. **Listen:** Consider a scenario where active listening led to a breakthrough in communication. How did it enhance your understanding of others' perspectives?

2. **Experiment:** Reflect on a situation where you initially hesitated due to fear of failure. How could embracing a mindset of experimentation and risk-taking have led to a different outcome?

Compelling Action Steps:

1. **Practice "Yes, And...":** In your next interaction, consciously apply the "Yes, And..." approach by accepting others' ideas and building upon them, fostering collaborative dialogue.

As Jake's journey with improv showed, the principles of The HONOR Code can find resonance in unexpected places. The power of "Yes, And..." and active listening transforms the dynamics of improvisation and holds the potential to reshape the landscape of leadership and collaboration. As you weave these principles into your daily interactions, remember that the journey towards alignment with The HONOR Code is ongoing, and each step you take contributes to the transformation of your leadership and the culture you nurture.

Chapter 13: Integrating Improv and Honor

With the seed of improvisation firmly planted in their minds, Jake and his team returned to Danalgo's headquarters, eager to weave the principles they learned into the fabric of their daily interactions. As days turned into weeks, the improv techniques began to take root, influencing their communication and their perspectives. The practice of "Yes, And..." became a mantra, fostering an environment where ideas were nurtured and explored, rather than shut down. Active listening, once a rarity, now became the foundation of every conversation, allowing each voice to be heard and valued.

For instance, the marketing team held their weekly meeting in a conference room at Danalgo headquarters. The atmosphere is tense as a disagreement about a new campaign escalates into a standoff between team members. The players in the mix are Jake, Megan (Head of Marketing), Alex (Senior Marketing Manager), and Lindsay (Creative Designer).

Megan: (frustrated) "I really think this new campaign should focus on our brand's artistic and creative side. It's what sets us apart!"

Alex: (defensive) "But Megan, data shows that our previous campaigns with a more analytical approach had a higher conversion rate. We need to stick with what works."

Lindsay: (trying to mediate) "Guys, let's not forget that both creativity and data-driven strategies have their merits. We need to find a way to balance them."

The tension in the room grows palpable as the conversation hits a deadlock. Megan and Alex are locked in a clash of viewpoints, each holding onto their stance firmly.

Jake: (interjecting with a calming tone) "Alright, I can see that we're passionate about this, and that's a good thing. Let's take a step back and see if we can find a middle ground."

Lindsay: (taking a deep breath) "Maybe we can consider combining both approaches. We could start with an eye-catching creative concept and then back it up with data-driven strategies for better targeting."

Megan: (softening her tone) "That's an interesting idea, Lindsay. It could be a way to appeal to both our artistic and analytical sides."

Alex: (nodding) "I see the value in that. We could also run some A/B tests to measure the effectiveness of different elements in the campaign."

Jake: (encouragingly) "I think we're onto something here. Megan, Alex, what do you both think about exploring this dual approach further?"

Megan: (with openness) "I'm willing to give it a shot, as long as we can monitor the results closely."

Alex: (agreeing) "Same here. Let's collaborate on designing a campaign that leverages both creativity and data."

Lindsay: (reflecting) "You know, I remember our improv workshop, where we learned to embrace each other's ideas. It's like practicing 'Yes, And...' in our meetings."

Jake: (smiling) "Absolutely, Lindsay. It's about acknowledging that every perspective contributes to the bigger picture."

Megan: (humbling herself) "I admit I was a bit stubborn about my approach. I appreciate both of you for challenging me."

Alex: (owning up) "And I should've been more open to considering creative elements. We're all learning."

Jake: (summing up) "This is what The HONOR Code is all about—collaborating, embracing diverse viewpoints, and finding solutions that benefit everyone. Let's move forward with this dual approach and stay committed to learning from the process."

The tension in the room has transformed into an atmosphere of collaboration and shared purpose. Through vulnerability, acknowledgment of mistakes, and collaborative problem-solving, the marketing team at Danalgo has bridged a conflict and demonstrated the principles they learned from improv—principles that resonate deeply with The HONOR Code.

As Jake led by example, openly sharing his thoughts and inviting input from all, a ripple effect cascaded through the organization. Maddy's guidance acted as a steady compass, ensuring that the principles of The HONOR Code remained at the heart of every interaction. Samantha's wisdom provided reassurance, reminding them that even in times of challenge, the journey toward Honor was a marathon, not a sprint.

Improv to Improve

The impact was profound on their professional relationships and their personal lives. Through embracing the tenets of improvisation, Jake and his team unlocked a pathway to empathy, compassion, and openness. And as they continued to explore this newfound terrain, the stage was set for a revelation—a connection between the art of improv and the core principles of The HONOR Code that was more significant than they could have ever imagined.

In the ever-evolving landscape of Danalgo, the integration of improv principles began to shine through, albeit not without its challenges. As the leaders attempted to apply "Yes, And..." and active listening, they found themselves navigating uncharted territory. One particularly memorable instance revealed the depth of this transformation as well as the remaining tensions.

Blaine, the Chief Operating Officer, maintained a skeptical stance toward the entire Honor Code initiative. The integration of improv into the equation stirred unease within him. He perceived the open and collaborative environment it generated as a potential challenge to his authority. Blaine's concerns centered around the notion that the improv approach might erode his control over certain aspects of the company. Jake and the rest of the leadership team were keenly aware of his perspective. Blaine's skepticism cast a shadow on their journey to increase Honor, and it appeared that this new phase was no exception.

The clash peaked during a pivotal strategy meeting. The team was brainstorming. However, Blaine's approach to this session was a departure from the "Yes, And..." principle they had been practicing. Instead of building upon ideas collaboratively, he discarded his colleagues' suggestions, with condescension. The tension in the room was tangible, a stark departure from the atmosphere of trust and collaboration they strived so hard to nurture.

In the midst of this charged environment, Samantha recognized the need to intervene. Leveraging the improv principles, she seized the opportunity to steer the discourse. Her voice, calm and composed, cut through the tension.

Samantha: (addressing the room) "Hey, let's take a moment here. I believe we're all on the same team, working towards the same goals. Blaine, your insights are invaluable. But I also think it's important that we listen to each other openly and build on ideas collaboratively. That's how we've been practicing the 'Yes, And...' approach, and it's helped us overcome challenges."

Blaine's skeptical gaze met Samantha's unwavering one. The room seemed to hold its breath.

Blaine: (pausing, then relenting) "You have a point, Samantha. I might have been too quick to dismiss ideas. It's just... change can be unsettling."

Samantha: (nodding) "Absolutely, change is uncomfortable. And... it's also an opportunity for growth. What if we apply the improv principle here? Instead of shutting down ideas, let's build on them together."

Blaine's initial resistance began to soften as Samantha's words resonated. The rest of the team sensed a shift in the atmosphere.

Jake: (supportively) "Samantha's right. The Honor Code isn't just about principles; it's about a culture we're striving to embody. A culture of collaboration, mutual respect, and continuous improvement."

The room's energy seemed to recalibrate. They started revisiting the dismissed ideas, this time allowing them to evolve and intertwine.

Marta: (enthusiastically) "What if we combine my proposal with Mark's idea? It could lead to a truly innovative approach!"

Blaine: (engaging) "I see potential in that collaboration. Let's explore it further."

Through Samantha's intervention and the application of improv principles, the meeting's trajectory shifted dramatically. What could have been a standoff turned into a catalyst for unity. The team collectively realized that the very principles they were advocating for could be instrumental in overcoming challenges, even when the challenge stemmed from within their own ranks.

The incident with Blaine served as a pivotal moment in the journey toward integrating improv techniques into their culture of Honor. It underscored the importance of addressing both external and internal resistance as they continued to reshape their interactions. Slowly but surely, the influence of "Yes, And..." began to permeate interactions beyond the leadership team, creating a ripple effect throughout the organization. What started as an experiment became standard for how they approached communication, collaboration, and problem-solving.

As the days turned into weeks, the impact of improv principles on Danalgo's culture became apparent. The notion of "Yes, And..." expanded beyond the walls of the leadership team's meetings, permeating interactions across departments and teams. Communication transformed into a collaborative dance, with team members building on each other's ideas and perspectives. Dismissive remarks or competitive undertones were replaced with genuine engagement and appreciation for diverse viewpoints.

Team dynamics also experienced a remarkable shift. Collaborative efforts were fueled by an inherent trust that grew through practicing "Yes, And..." and active listening. The initial hesitance to share thoughts was replaced by a sense of psychological safety, allowing individuals to voice their opinions without fear of ridicule or judgment. This newfound camaraderie led to more creative problem-solving and innovative solutions that had previously been hindered by the fear of stepping outside the status quo.

Reflections 3-2-1

Lessons Learned: In this chapter, we explored the integration of improv techniques and the Honor Code principles into the fabric of Danalgo's culture. We learned that combining the art of improvisation with the pursuit of Honor can foster a collaborative environment, enhance communication skills, and inspire empathetic leadership.

Key Takeaways:

1. **Integration of Principles:** The integration of improv principles into the Honor Code journey has shown how seemingly unrelated concepts can harmonize to create a culture of collaboration and growth.

2. **Transformation through Collaboration:** The experience with the marketing team exemplified the potential for improv techniques to defuse conflicts, encourage active listening, and drive collaborative problem-solving.

3. **Catalyzing Change:** The skepticism and resistance encountered within the organization reflect the challenges of embracing change. However, these obstacles can be transformed into opportunities for growth and development.

Reflective Questions:

1. **Applying Improv:** How can you apply the "Yes, And..." and active listening principles to your interactions, fostering a more open and collaborative atmosphere?

2. **Navigating Resistance:** Have you encountered resistance to change, either externally or within yourself? How can you approach such resistance with the spirit of growth and openness?

Compelling Action Steps:

1. **Embrace Vulnerability:** Identify a situation where acknowledging your own mistakes and seeking solutions collaboratively can foster trust and enhance team dynamics.

In the journey of integrating improv and the Honor Code, Jake and his team have experienced synergy. By embracing the principles of improvisation, they have nurtured a culture where diverse ideas are welcomed, active listening is paramount, and vulnerability is celebrated. The challenges they encountered called for perseverance in the face of resistance, and a collaborative spirit flowed throughout the organization.

As Jake, Maddy, and the team ventured deeper into this uncharted territory, the lessons learned from improv resonated far beyond the stage. The connection between improvisation and the Honor Code principles revealed itself to be profound. With each interaction infused with the spirit of "Yes, And...", Danalgo's journey toward a culture of Honor and collaboration continued, inspiring both leaders and employees to reach new heights of understanding, empathy, and achievement.

Chapter 14: Leading with Empathy

As the culture of collaboration and open communication continued to flourish, a change was emerging within the leadership team – one that aligned with the HONOR Code's principle of "Others' Focus." The shift wasn't just in behavior but in mindset. The leaders experienced the power of empathy building strong relationships and effective teams. As they embraced the value of understanding and considering the perspectives and feelings of others, they were better equipped to lead with compassion.

With each passing day, the transformation of the Danalgo leadership team was more evident. The principles of the HONOR Code took root in their actions, decisions, and interactions. They embraced empathy as a core element of their leadership style, and their ability to connect with employees on a deeper level grew. The once-formidable barriers between leadership and staff started to dissolve, replaced by a sense of unity and shared purpose.

Empathy became a guiding light, illuminating the path to more meaningful and impactful leadership. The leaders were no longer content with surface-level conversations; they sought to understand their employees' experiences, challenges, and aspirations. By actively listening and showing genuine care for their team members, they fostered an environment of trust and support that would propel the organization to new heights.

Jake made time to engage in one-on-one conversations with employees from various departments. He learned about their day-to-day experiences, their goals, and their personal lives. During one of these conversations, he discovered an employee's passion for community service. That sparked an idea that would enhance the company's impact on the community and align with the HONOR Code's principle of "Offerings."

As Jake shared his vision with Maddy and Samantha, they wholeheartedly embraced the concept. They began to explore ways in which Danalgo could contribute to the community through volunteer initiatives and charitable partnerships. By leading with empathy, Jake uncovered a way to enrich the lives of his employees and extend Danalgo's positive influence beyond its walls.

In their pursuit of empathetic leadership, the Danalgo team entered new territory. They recognized that in order to truly understand their employees' perspectives and experiences, they needed to step out of their comfort zones and approach things from a different angle. This is where the power of improv techniques came into play.

Making It Real

The leaders organized a series of interactive workshops for their employees. These workshops incorporated various improv techniques that would encourage open communication, active listening, and a deeper understanding of one another. Jake, Maddy, and Samantha participated alongside their team members, eager to learn and grow together.

One of the exercises they engaged in was a role reversal scenario. Each leader was paired with an employee from a different department and tasked with taking on the other person's role for a day. This experience allowed them to gain firsthand insight into the challenges, responsibilities, and perspectives of their colleagues. As Jake stepped into the shoes of a customer service representative, he realized the unique pressures they faced and the importance of addressing customer concerns with empathy and urgency.

Another exercise centered around the "Yes, And..." principle. Participants were encouraged to build upon each other's ideas in a spontaneous and collaborative manner. As the leaders and employees contributed their thoughts, they experienced a heightened sense of teamwork and creativity. Blaine initially struggled with this exercise. His tendency to be dismissive of others' ideas clashed with the core principle of building upon them. Through patient coaching from Maddy and supportive interactions with his team, Blaine gradually opened up to the "Yes, And..." mindset, realizing its potential to foster acceptance and innovation.

Reflections 3-2-1

Lessons Learned: In this chapter, we delved into the concept of empathetic leadership and its integration into the evolving culture at Danalgo. We learned that leading with empathy forges stronger relationships, effective teams, and aligns harmoniously with the "Others' Focus" principle of the HONOR Code.

Key Takeaways:

1. **Empathy as Transformation:** The embrace of empathy by the leadership team at Danalgo showcases the profound impact it can have on organizational culture and relationships.

2. **Building Unity through Understanding:** The leaders' commitment to understanding employees' experiences and perspectives has dismantled barriers, fostering unity and shared purpose.

3. **Empathy's Ripple Effect:** Leading with empathy has catalyzed the growth of trust and support, laying the foundation for impactful leadership and extending the organization's positive influence.

Reflective Questions:

1. **Empathetic Engagement:** How can you actively engage with your team members to better understand their experiences and perspectives? What steps can you take to make genuine connections?

2. **Overcoming Comfort Zones:** Reflect on a situation where you stepped out of your comfort zone to gain a different perspective. How did this experience enhance your understanding and leadership capabilities?

Compelling Action Steps:

1. **Role Reversal:** Organize an activity that encourages role reversal within your team, allowing each member to gain insight into the perspectives and responsibilities of their colleagues.

As the leaders of Danalgo incorporated empathy into their leadership style, a transformation took place. Their actions resonated with the core principles of the HONOR Code, valuing others and their perspectives. By actively understand their employees' experiences and engaging in open and authentic conversations, the leaders created an atmosphere of trust, support, and shared growth.

Through workshops and improv techniques, the leaders immersed themselves in the experiences of their team members. Role reversal and collaborative exercises highlighted the power of empathy in fostering understanding and innovation. Even those initially resistant to change, like Blaine, found themselves opening up to new mindsets that nurtured acceptance and teamwork.

As the journey continued, the Danalgo leadership team recognized that empathetic leadership wasn't just a fleeting trend but an essential aspect of their legacy. Through empathetic engagement they reinforced the principles of the HONOR Code in a tangible and transformative manner. By learning from each other and encouraging a culture of empathy, they shaped their organization's trajectory and made a lasting impact on their people and the broader community.

Chapter 15: Community Leaders

As the influence of the HONOR Code extended beyond the confines of the corporate setting, the Danalgo team recognized the potential for its principles to benefit the broader community. The same values and practices that transformed their leadership could be applied to strengthen community bonds and create an environment of acceptance and collaboration.

Collaborating with Community Leaders

Jake, Maddy, Samantha, and a group of enthusiastic employees embarked on a new initiative—callaborate with local community leaders. Their goal was to introduce improv techniques to community organizations, schools, and non-profits to promote understanding, empathy, and teamwork among diverse groups of people.

They partnered with a youth center that provided after-school programs for children from different backgrounds. Together with the community leaders, they designed improv-based activities that encouraged the children to work together, express their ideas, and actively listen to one another. Through these activities, the children learned to appreciate one another's unique perspectives and to build upon each other's contributions, embodying the spirit of "Yes, And..."

At a local neighborhood association meeting, they facilitated an improv-inspired discussion about community development. By using improv techniques, the residents felt more comfortable sharing their thoughts, and the atmosphere shifted from a formal meeting to an engaging conversation. Even Blaine found himself participating actively, realizing that the principles of improv transcended professional contexts and were equally relevant in community interactions.

As the influence of the HONOR Code extended beyond the corporate setting, the Danalgo team recognized the potential for its principles to benefit the broader community. They understood that the same values and practices that transformed their leadership could strengthen community bonds and create an environment of acceptance and collaboration.

Improv Can Break Down Barriers

In their journey to foster acceptance, Jake and his team encountered a local organization that provided support to refugees and immigrants. The organization faced challenges in integrating newcomers into the community and breaking down the cultural barriers that often led to misunderstanding and isolation.

The Danalgo team collaborated with the organization to design improv workshops tailored to the diverse group of participants. Through carefully crafted activities, participants were encouraged to share their personal stories and experiences while practicing active listening and empathy. The improv sessions created an atmosphere of mutual respect, where participants felt heard and valued regardless of their backgrounds.

During one improv exercise where participants were tasked with finishing each other's sentences, Jake found himself paired with a young woman who recently arrived as a refugee. As they completed each other's sentences, they discovered shared aspirations and common challenges, transcending language and cultural barriers.

> **Young Woman:** (smiling) "Nuestros sueños, son como estrellas..."
> **Translator:** "Our dreams, they are like stars..."
> **Jake:** (joining in) "...guiding us through the darkest nights."

Translator: "...guiándonos a través de las noches más oscuras."
Young Woman: (nodding) "Y los desafíos a los que nos enfrentamos..."
Translator: "And the challenges we face..."
Jake: (finishing) "...are the winds that make us stronger."
Translator: "Nuestros sueños, son como estrellas..."

The experience left Jake with a sense of connection and a renewed dedication to fostering acceptance. In those shared moments of creativity and understanding, they bridged the gaps that words alone couldn't reach.

Reflections 3-2-1

Lessons Learned: In this chapter, we extended the principles of the HONOR Code into the broader community. Through the integration of improv techniques, we learned to foster acceptance and collaboration among diverse groups of people.

Key Takeaways:

1. **Community Impact of the HONOR Code:** We discovered that the values and practices of the HONOR Code have a transformative potential that reaches far beyond the walls of a corporate setting. The principles of empathy, active listening, and collaboration can help strengthen community bonds and create a culture of acceptance.

2. **Improv as a Catalyst for Change:** improv techniques proved to be powerful catalysts for breaking down barriers and encouraging meaningful interactions. Improv-based activities provided a safe and engaging platform for people from different backgrounds to share their perspectives and stories, leading to mutual understanding and connection.

3. **Shared Humanity Through Creativity:** The experiences of transcending language and cultural barriers through improv exercises highlighted the universal aspects of the human experience. Creativity became a bridge that connected individuals, allowing them to see beyond their differences and discover shared aspirations and challenges.

Reflective Questions:

1. **Foster Acceptance:** How can the principles of empathy and collaboration promoted by the HONOR Code be applied in your local community or organization to foster acceptance and understanding among diverse groups?

2. **Active Listening:** Consider an instance when you actively listened to someone from a different background and learned something new. How can you incorporate this practice into your daily life to promote acceptance and enrich your understanding of others?

Compelling Action Steps:

1. **Community Outreach:** Identify local organizations or groups that could benefit from the principles of the HONOR Code and improv techniques. Explore opportunities to collaborate on workshops or events that promote acceptance, empathy, and collaboration.

By extending the reach of the HONOR Code and embracing the lessons learned from improv, we can create positive ripples that transcend boundaries and transform communities. As we continue to explore the intersections of empathy, creativity, and collaboration, we contribute to building a world where acceptance and understanding flourish, enriching our lives and the lives of those around us.

Chapter 16: Government Leaders

As the HONOR Code continued to ripple outward, its impact reached even the highest echelons of government leadership. Government officials, faced with the responsibility of transparently communicating with their constituents and making decisions that would shape the lives of many, found inspiration in the principles of the HONOR Code.

Transparent Collaboration

Jake and his team were invited to collaborate with a group of government leaders who recognized the need for improved communication and transparency in their interactions with the public. They were grappling with the challenge of addressing citizens' concerns and building trust in an environment often marked by skepticism and cynicism.

The Danalgo team introduced the government leaders to the world of improv, explaining how the practice could foster authenticity, active listening, and open dialogue. With cautious optimism, the government officials participated in a series of improv workshops designed to simulate real-world scenarios they faced in their roles.

One exercise involved the officials taking turns delivering public statements about contentious issues, while their colleagues improvised questions and challenges from the perspective of concerned citizens. Through this exercise, the government leaders experienced firsthand the importance of empathetic listening and addressing constituents' concerns directly.

The experience was transformative. As government officials embraced the principles of improv, they noticed a shift in their communication style. They began to prioritize listening over speaking, engage in more constructive dialogue, and acknowledge the validity of differing perspectives.

With their newfound improv-inspired communication skills, the government leaders embarked on a path of transparency and collaboration. They recognized that effective leadership was not just about delivering messages, but about creating an environment where citizens felt heard, valued, and informed.

As the HONOR Code continued to ripple outward, its impact reached even the highest echelons of government leadership. Government officials, faced with the responsibility of transparently communicating with their constituents and making decisions that would shape the lives of many, found inspiration in the principles of the HONOR Code.

Making a Daily Difference

The government leaders didn't stop at mere workshop exercises; they embraced improv principles in their daily interactions with the public and their colleagues. One instance that highlighted the power of these principles occurred during a town hall meeting focused on a controversial urban development project.

In the past, such meetings often devolved into heated arguments and frustrated citizens leaving without feeling heard. However, armed with their newfound improv skills, the government officials approached the meeting differently. They employed the "Yes, And..." technique to acknowledge citizens' concerns while also presenting their own perspectives.

When a concerned citizen voiced worries about the impact of the development on local businesses, a government leader responded with "Yes, And... we're actively working to ensure that local businesses have a voice in the planning process." This simple shift in language, from defensiveness to collaboration, transformed the atmosphere of the meeting.

The government leaders also utilized active listening techniques, showing genuine empathy for the residents' stories and concerns.

Instead of immediately offering solutions, they allowed citizens to express themselves fully, creating an environment of trust and open dialogue.

The result was a town hall meeting that addressed citizens' concerns and fostered a sense of community and shared purpose. Citizens left feeling that their voices had been heard, even if solutions weren't immediate. This shift in communication style led to more effective public discourse and decision-making, highlighting the potential of improv techniques to transform even the most challenging interactions.

Reflections 3-2-1

Lessons Learned: In this chapter, we applied the principles of the HONOR Code to government leadership and transparent communication. Through the integration of improv techniques, we learned that these principles can enhance authenticity, active listening, and open dialogue, leading to more effective governance and citizen engagement.

Key Takeaways:

1. **Government Transparency through Empathy:** We discovered that the principles of the HONOR Code are not confined to business settings. Government leaders can use empathy and active listening to transform their communication style, fostering transparency, understanding, and trust among their constituents.

2. **Improving Public Discourse:** The utilization of improv techniques, such as "Yes, And..." and active listening, can impact public interactions. By employing these techniques, government officials can create an environment where diverse perspectives are acknowledged, leading to more constructive and collaborative public discourse.

3. **Empowering Meaningful Engagement:** The integration of improv principles into government leadership encourages citizen engagement. By genuinely addressing concerns and demonstrating empathy, government leaders can empower citizens to participate fully.

Reflective Questions:

1. **Transformative Listening:** Think of a situation where active listening transformed a challenging interaction into a productive dialogue. How can this approach be integrated into government meetings or town hall discussions to build trust and understanding?

2. **Empathetic Decisions:** Consider a time when you witnessed the positive impact of a government decision that prioritized empathy and collaboration. How can you contribute to promoting such practices in your role as a citizen?

Compelling Action Steps:

1. **Government Workshop Initiatives:** Collaborate with local government organizations to introduce improv-based workshops that focus on transparent communication and active listening. Provide practical tools for government officials to enhance their interactions with constituents.

By recognizing the potential of the HONOR Code principles and improv techniques in government leadership, we can transform the way decisions are made and communities are shaped. Embracing empathy, active listening, and collaboration within government settings can lead to effective governance, enhanced citizen engagement, and a harmonious society. As we continue to explore these intersections, we contribute to the realization of a government that truly serves and empowers its people.

Chapter 17: The Power of Reflection

With each step of their transformative journey, the leaders came to understand the immense power of reflection. It was a practice that connected the dots between their individual experiences, the principles of the HONOR Code, and the impact they were making on their organizations, communities, and families.

Reflect a Better Future

Jake, Maddy, and the others didn't view reflection as a mere routine, but rather as a compass guiding their actions and decisions. As the leader of Danalgo, Jake made it a habit to set aside time at the end of each day to reflect on his interactions, decisions, and the alignment of his actions with the HONOR Code. This introspective practice allowed him to continually fine-tune his leadership approach and identify areas where he could better embody the Code's principles.

Maddy observed Jake's growth with a sense of pride. As the Guide, she witnessed firsthand how his dedication to reflection brought about shifts in his leadership style. His conversations with Maddy often centered around his discoveries during these reflective moments, leading to deeper insights and a stronger connection between theory and practice.

Across the organizations they touched, leaders incorporated reflection as an essential tool for growth. In boardrooms, team meetings, and family discussions, the practice of reflection became a catalyst for open conversations. Even Blaine, whose resistance to the HONOR Code was a constant source of tension, found himself engaging in moments of introspection.

As Jake shared his reflections with his mentor Samantha Knight, she noted that reflection was a pillar of his continued Honor. "Reflection," she said, "gives us the space to align our actions with our intentions, to recognize the moments when we fall short of our ideals, and to actively choose to course-correct."

Maddy agreed, adding, "Reflection bridges the gap between who we are and who we aspire to be. It's where our journey meets our destination."

The Brain Reflects

The insights from neuroscience and the principles of improv wove themselves into the fabric of the leaders' journey, and reflection served as the thread that stitched it all together. The symposium's revelations about cognitive load theory, mirror neurons, and emotional engagement found resonance in their reflective practices.

Jake found himself contemplating the neuroscience behind empathy, realizing how understanding the workings of mirror neurons deepened his Others-Focus. Maddy, too, recognized that the neurological foundation of emotional engagement underscored the importance of genuine interactions and the positive influence they had on shaping organizational culture.

As they discussed these connections, Maddy shared a story about a moment of deep empathy she experienced during an improv exercise. "When you truly listen and build upon your scene partner's contribution in improv, it's like activating mirror neurons of empathy," she explained. "You're attuning yourself to their emotions and offering support, just as we do when we prioritize Others-Focus."

Jake nodded in agreement. "And it's not just about the individual," he added. "When we create an environment where emotional engagement and empathetic interactions are the norm, we're fostering a culture where the collective becomes stronger than the sum of its parts."

Reflections 3-2-1

Lessons Learned: In this chapter, we explored the impact of reflection, weaving it into the journey of transformation guided by the HONOR Code. Through the integration of introspection, we uncovered how reflection connected our experiences, the Code's tenets, and the ripple effects of our actions across organizations, communities, and personal lives.

Key Takeaways:

1. **Reflection as a Compass:** We discovered that reflection is a compass that navigates the alignment between our intentions and actions. Leaders like Jake and Maddy harnessed reflection to fine-tune their leadership approaches to foster alignment with the HONOR Code.

2. **Catalyst for Open Conversations:** Reflection became a catalyst for open conversations within the boardrooms, team meetings, and in personal settings. Reflection creates space for dialogue, course correction, and a deeper understanding of each other's perspectives.

3. **Bridging Journey and Destination:** The practice of reflection bridged the gap between our present selves and our aspirational ideals. It facilitated a connection between where we stand and where we aim to be.

Reflective Questions:

1. **Reflect to Align:** Reflect on a recent interaction or decision. How did practicing reflection help you align your actions with the principles of the HONOR Code?

2. **Reflect to Course Correct:** Consider a challenging situation where you were able to course-correct through reflection. How can you encourage others to embrace reflective practices for continuous growth?

Compelling Action Steps:

1. **Daily Reflection Ritual:** Incorporate a daily practice of reflection into your routine. Allocate time to review your interactions, decisions, and alignment with the HONOR Code. Use this practice to identify areas for improvement and celebrate moments of alignment.

Through the lens of reflection, we have seen the intricate interplay of neuroscience insights and improv principles. Look inward to create meaningful outward impacts. Reflection fosters growth, alignment, and empathy. Reflect to embody the HONOR Code in each facet of your life.

Chapter 18: Overcoming Personal Struggles

Tested by Struggles

Life is an intricate tapestry woven with threads of challenges and triumphs, and the leaders in this journey were no exception. Each had their own personal struggles that tested their commitment to the HONOR Code and pushed them to seek growth.

Samantha Knight faced a family crisis that shook her to her core. Her parents lived in a peaceful coastal town that was suddenly in the aftermath of a devastating natural disaster, a scene of destruction and chaos. Samantha's family home, along with many others, was ravaged by the powerful forces of nature, leaving behind a landscape of broken memories.

During these heart-wrenching moments of vulnerability, Samantha turned to the principle of Reflection. As she looked inward, the waves of her emotions and motivations became clear. With every thought, she felt a surge of love for her family, a determination to support them, and a sense of responsibility to lead through the crisis.

Her Non-Negotiables became a guiding light. As Samantha navigated the difficult decisions that lay ahead, the HONOR Code acted as an unwavering anchor. In the face of adversity, she found comfort in the truth, drawing strength from her commitment to integrity even in the most challenging circumstances. Empathy, a pillar of her character, allowed her to stand in her parents' shoes, understanding their fears and hopes as they faced the aftermath of the disaster.

Amidst the chaos, accountability resonated profoundly. Samantha recognized that she held a responsibility to her family and to herself. This commitment to accountability empowered her to take decisive actions, rallying support for her parents and their community, and ensuring that they weren't alone in their journey of recovery.

As Samantha reflected on her experiences, she discovered a newfound resilience within herself. The practice of reflection allowed her to process her emotions and see her path forward. Through the storms, she emerged stronger, guided by the unwavering principles that defined her character. Just as the devastation could not erase the beauty of the coastal town, the crisis could not erode the core values that Samantha held dear.

On the other hand, Blaine DeShield's struggles were fueled by his ambition and ego. His desire to seize power at any cost led him to make ethically questionable decisions that contradicted the principles of the HONOR Code. However, the code's emphasis on positive influence and support highlighted the path of redemption. Through self-reflection, Blaine recognized the impact of his actions on others and began to see the value in building relationships based on trust and respect.

As for Jake, his personal struggle emerged from his deep-seated fear of failure. The pressure to lead a transformative change and his internal doubts threatened to derail his commitment to the HONOR Code. Yet, his reflection revealed the importance of cultivating positive Habits to overcome adversity. With each setback, he consciously practiced resilience and perseverance, demonstrating that even in moments of uncertainty, the HONOR Code was a guiding light.

Maddy Davidson, the Guide, shared her insights as well. "Life's challenges can either break us or shape us," she said. "When we apply the HONOR Code to our struggles, they become opportunities for growth. Each principle offers a lens through which we can navigate difficulties with integrity and empathy."

The Tools to Overcome

The journey of these leaders was not without its trials, but the fusion of neuroscience insights and improv tools provided them with a powerful toolkit to confront and conquer obstacles.

As Samantha navigated her family crisis, she harnessed the knowledge of cognitive load theory to manage the overwhelming emotions that threatened her judgment. Understanding the brain's capacity for processing information enabled her to approach decisions with clarity and rationality, even amidst chaos.

Jake, drawing on his experience in the improv workshop, embraced the principle of "Yes, And..." in his internal dialogue. Instead of succumbing to self-doubt, he acknowledged his fears and weaknesses ("Yes") and then built upon them with positive affirmations and proactive actions ("And..."). This mental shift empowered him to face challenges head-on and adapt with resilience.

Blaine, at a crossroads of Honorable decision-making, utilized mirror neurons to develop empathy for those affected by his choices. He recognized that by understanding others' perspectives, he could reshape his behavior and contribute positively to his relationships and the organization.

Maddy Davidson interjected, "When we combine the cognitive insights of neuroscience with the adaptive thinking of improv, we equip ourselves with the tools needed to rise above personal struggles. It's about rewiring our thought patterns, breaking down mental barriers, and fostering empathetic connections."

Reflections 3-2-1

Lessons Learned: In this chapter, we learn to overcome personal struggles. Challenges, though daunting, can serve as transformative opportunities for growth and self-discovery. By applying the principles of the HONOR Code, neuroscience insights, and the adaptive strategies of improv, our leaders displayed the resilience of the human spirit.

Key Takeaways:

1. **Resilience Through Reflection:** Personal struggles can be navigated with strength and resilience when approached through the lens of introspection and reflection. In the face of adversity, the practice of reflecting on our values and principles becomes an essential compass guiding our decisions and actions.

2. **Empathy and Positive Influence:** The power of empathy and positive influence emerged as transformative forces in overcoming personal challenges. By stepping into the shoes of others and understanding their perspectives, we can reframe our behavior and forge stronger, more meaningful connections.

3. **Tools for Triumph:** Neuroscience insights and improv techniques provide a toolkit for conquering obstacles. Understanding cognitive load theory helps us manage overwhelming emotions, while the "Yes, And..." principle equips us to confront self-doubt and uncertainty. Leveraging mirror neurons enables us to foster empathy and reshape our interactions with others.

Reflective Questions:

1. **Yes, and…:** Reflect on a time when you faced self-doubt. How could the "Yes, And..." principle have empowered you to overcome it?

2. **Guided by Neuroscience:** How can you apply neuroscience insights to manage overwhelming emotions during challenging times, and how might this influence your decision-making process?

Compelling Action Steps:

1. **Embrace Empathetic Listening:** Engage in conversations with those who have faced similar struggles. Practice active empathy by truly understanding their experiences and leverage their insights to navigate your own challenges with greater compassion.

As we close this chapter, let's remember that life's struggles are not roadblocks but stepping stones to growth. By employing the principles of the HONOR Code, neuroscience, and improv, we have the tools to emerge from challenges stronger, wiser, and more connected than ever before.

HONOR Becomes the Standard

The transformation within Danalgo was palpable. The HONOR Code evolved from a novel concept to a fundamental of the company's identity. As the months rolled on, leaders found themselves instinctively applying the principles of Habits, Offerings, Non-Negotiables, Others-Focus, and Reflection to their daily routines, interactions, and decision-making processes.

Jake McLeash observed with a sense of satisfaction as his leadership team engaged in open dialogues guided by empathy and respect. Blaine DeShield, once a skeptic of the HONOR project, became a willing participant in team-building exercises that fostered collaboration and cohesion. The energy within the organization shifted from mere compliance to belief in the power of Honor to drive positive change.

Samantha Knight beamed with pride as she witnessed the impact on the company's culture and its bottom line. Employee morale soared, attrition rates plummeted, and creativity flourished as the once-isolated workforce found unity and camaraderie in their shared Honor.

The transformation was more than a mere trend—it was a movement. Maddy Davidson remarked, "When Honor becomes a way of life, organizations flourish. It's the conscious choice to uphold values, the sincere commitment to growth, and the unwavering dedication to serving others that create an ecosystem where Honor thrives."

As the organization consistently applied the principles of the HONOR Code, their actions aligned seamlessly with the acronym—Habits, Offerings, Non-Negotiables, Others-Focus, and Reflection. Their journey culminated in a culture marked by Honor and sustained by their unyielding dedication.

Habits Stick

The impact of the HONOR Code on Danalgo's success went far beyond the bottom line. The organizational transformation left an indelible mark on every aspect of its existence. As leaders applied the principles, the ripple effects reached employee well-being and community engagement.

Employee well-being soared as individuals felt valued and respected within the workplace. The company became a safe haven, where employees could express their ideas openly, knowing that their perspectives were heard and embraced. The culture of Honor eradicated toxic competition and replaced it with support and collaboration. Employees woke up excited to contribute their offerings to a company that reciprocated with growth, opportunity, and a sense of belonging.

The transformation extended beyond the office walls. The community that surrounded Danalgo reaped the benefits of its leaders' Honor. The company engaged in local initiatives, addressing societal challenges with innovative solutions. They hosted workshops, volunteered at schools, and organized events that fostered unity and growth. As Jake McLeash once said, "The success of a company isn't just measured in profits—it's measured in the positive change it brings to its community."

Through their dedication to the HONOR Code, the leaders understood the impact of their actions was not confined to the office or the boardroom. Their Honor had a far-reaching influence that touched the lives of employees, families, and the community at large.

Reflections 3-2-1

Lessons Learned: In this chapter, we embarked on a journey of sustaining transformative by embodying the HONOR Code. We learned that when values become habits and principles are consistently applied, a culture of Honor emerges and flourishes, impacting individuals, organizations, and communities.

Key Takeaways:

1. **Culture of Honor:** The journey from introducing the HONOR Code to embodying it as a way of life is marked by shifts in culture. When the principles of Habits, Offerings, Non-Negotiables, Others-Focus, and Reflection are integrated into everyday actions, a culture of Honor fosters unity, collaboration, and growth.

2. **Beyond the Bottom Line:** The transformation caused by the HONOR Code transcends financial metrics. A workplace that embodies Honor supports employee well-being, where every voice is heard, and toxic competition is replaced by support and unity. This culture extends beyond the organization and contributes positively to the surrounding community.

3. **Creating Positive Change:** The impact of Honor goes beyond the office walls, touching lives within and beyond the organization. By practicing Honor, leaders can effect change in their community, addressing challenges, fostering unity, and leaving a lasting legacy of growth and empathy.

Reflective Questions:

1. **Impact:** How have the principles of the HONOR Code transformed your daily routines, interactions, and decision-making processes?

2. **Reach:** In what ways can you extend the principles of Honor beyond your immediate environment to create positive change in your community?

Compelling Action Steps:

1. **Extend the Ripple:** Embrace the role of a positive influencer in your community. Organize initiatives that reflect the values of Honor—foster unity, address challenges, and contribute to growth.

As we conclude this journey, let's remember that the transformation from concept to culture is a testament to the power of commitment and consistency. By sustaining the principles of the HONOR Code, we uphold the values that lead to unity, growth, and positive change.

Chapter 20: The Legacy of Transformation

An Honorable Heritage

As time passed, the transformation that took root within Danalgo continued to flourish, solidifying its place in the annals of organizational history. The legacy of the leaders' journey was imprinted on the DNA of the company, shaping its culture, values, and interactions. The HONOR Code became a testament to the power of positive leadership and its capacity to bring about lasting change.

Jake McLeash, once a skeptic, became a true believer in the HONOR Code. His unwavering Honor secured his role as CEO and ignited a cultural revolution that rippled through every department. Employees embraced the five pillars with enthusiasm, crafting habits that promoted collaboration, extending offerings that enriched the workplace, and upholding non-negotiables that kept the company's integrity intact.

Maddy Davidson's guidance sparked the transformation at Danalgo and laid the foundation for a new era of leadership. Her tireless efforts transformed her role from a guide to a mentor, fostering the growth of leaders who carry the torch of Honor forward. The lessons learned through the journey were absorbed intellectually and internalized deeply, becoming a part of the leaders' essence.

Samantha Knight's influence continued to serve as a guiding light. Her wisdom provided the framework for Jake's journey, and her support fortified his resolve during the toughest times. The partnership between mentor and mentee blossomed into a friendship rooted in shared values and a mutual commitment to the betterment of the organization.

Through their collective effort, the leaders uncovered a universal truth: that the HONOR Code was a set of principles to follow and a way of life to embrace. By embodying these principles, they transformed their company into a beacon of Honor, a place where respect, integrity, and empathy were the driving forces behind every decision and interaction.

Sharing Honor

The transformation of Danalgo's culture into a bastion of Honor was not confined within the company's walls; it radiated outward. The once-skeptical employees, now fervent advocates of the HONOR Code, carried its principles into their homes, families, and communities. The ripple effect of their commitment was undeniable, and it wasn't long before others took notice.

As Danalgo's reputation for Honorable leadership and a values-driven culture spread, it attracted attention from other organizations seeking to follow a similar path. Competitors, clients, and even other industries began to take cues from Danalgo's journey, realizing that the HONOR Code was a blueprint for creating sustainable success and fostering positive change.

Leaders from different companies sought Jake's advice, attended workshops led by Maddy Davidson, and engaged in dialogues with Samantha Knight about their own journeys toward Honor. The principles that ignited a transformation within Danalgo sparked a movement, with leaders from various sectors embracing the HONOR Code as a way to drive positive change in their organizations and beyond.

The leaders of Danalgo unwittingly became champions of a movement—a movement rooted in Honor, integrity, and positive leadership. The legacy of their journey transcended their own organization, leaving an indelible mark on the business landscape and inspiring others to walk the path of Honor.

The Movement Takes Off

The seeds of transformation that took root within Danalgo blossomed into a movement dedicated to fostering Honor in all aspects of life. As the principles of the HONOR Code became ingrained in the hearts and minds of Danalgo's leaders and employees, they felt compelled to share their experiences and insights with the world.

Jake, Maddy, and Samantha embarked on a mission to spread the principles of Honor beyond the boundaries of their company. They realized the impact of their journey could be magnified by influencing other organizations, communities, and even society. The Honor Movement was born—grounded in the belief that when individuals and organizations prioritize Honor, the ripple effect of positive change extends far and wide.

Under the banner of the Honor Movement, workshops, seminars, and conferences were organized to share the insights gained from Danalgo's transformation. Leaders from various industries gathered to learn how to implement the HONOR Code principles within their own organizations, from startups to established corporations. The movement transcended sector boundaries, uniting leaders from technology, healthcare, education, and more, all seeking to embrace a Honor-driven approach to leadership.

The Honor Movement taught the leaders of Danalgo a powerful lesson—a culture of Honor has implications far beyond their immediate surroundings. By courageously sharing their challenges, successes, and the principles that guided them, they catalyzed a wider cultural shift. Their experience proved that the impact of leadership extends well beyond the confines of individual organizations, shaping the way business is conducted on a larger scale.

The Movement Gains Momentum

As the Honor Movement gained momentum, the leaders of Danalgo recognized the importance of collaboration and partnership in creating a lasting impact. To influence positive change on a global scale, they connected with other entities that shared their vision of promoting Honor, ethics, and positive leadership.

Jake, Maddy, and Samantha reached out to like-hearted organizations, both within and beyond the business realm. They formed alliances with educational institutions, non-profit organizations, government agencies, and even international corporations that were committed to fostering a culture of Honor and integrity. Through these collaborations, they leveraged their collective resources, knowledge, and influence to create a network dedicated to the advancement of Honorable leadership.

Together with their partners, the leaders of Danalgo launched initiatives that aimed to spread the principles of the HONOR Code across borders. They developed educational programs that integrated the Code's teachings into school curricula, nurturing the next generation of leaders with a strong foundation of Honor and integrity. They worked with government agencies to advocate for policies that promoted Honorable conduct and transparency in both public and private sectors.

Across industries and continents, the Honor Movement's message resonated with individuals and organizations seeking to make a positive impact. Leaders from all walks of life came together to share their stories, exchange insights, and collaborate on projects that aligned with the Code's principles. The movement became a force for change, inspiring individuals to rethink their approach to leadership and encouraging them to embrace a more Honorable way of living and working.

Through their collaboration with diverse entities, the leaders of Danalgo realized the immense potential of unity in driving meaningful change. The Honor Movement demonstrated that when individuals and organizations join forces to pursue a common goal, their collective impact is far greater than the sum of their individual efforts. By fostering a sense of shared purpose and interconnectedness, they were able to effect change on a global scale.

Reflections 3-2-1

Lessons Learned: In this chapter, we delved into the culmination of the transformative journey within Danalgo—the birth of the Honor Movement. By embodying the HONOR Code's principles and sharing their experiences, leaders can spark a movement that extends beyond their organization.

Key Takeaways:

1. **Legacy of Honor:** The journey of transformation within Danalgo left an indelible mark on the company's culture, values, and interactions. The HONOR Code became a living testament to the power of positive leadership, serving as a blueprint for creating lasting change.

2. **Ripple Effect:** The transformation within Danalgo impacted employees, families, and communities. The embodiment of Honor within the company inspired advocates who carried its principles into their homes and extended the ripple of positive change.

3. **The Birth of a Movement:** The Honor Movement emerged as a natural evolution of Danalgo's transformation, driven by the leaders' commitment to sharing their insights and experiences. This movement galvanized leaders across industries, uniting them in their pursuit of Honorable leadership and ethics.

Reflective Questions:

1. **Extend Beyond:** Consider a time when you witnessed the ripple effect of positive change extending beyond your workplace into your community. How did the principles of the HONOR Code play a role in fostering this broader impact?

2. **Inspire Others:** In what ways can you contribute to the Honor Movement and promote positive change in your industry or community? How might you share your experiences and insights to inspire others to embrace the principles of Honor?

Compelling Action Steps:

1. **Champion Positive Leadership:** Continue to exemplify the principles of the HONOR Code within your organization. Share your experiences with others and encourage them to embrace a culture of Honor, integrity, and positive leadership.

As we reflect on the legacy of transformation within Danalgo and the birth of the Honor Movement, let's remember that the impact of Honorable leadership knows no bounds. By sharing our experiences, insights, and commitment to Honor, we have the power to shape a better future for organizations, communities, and the world at large.

Conclusion: A New Era of Leadership

Honor is at the Core of Transformation

Looking back on their experiences, they recognized that the true essence of leadership lay in the alignment of their actions with the core values of Honor, integrity, and empathy. Through the practice of fostering positive **habits**, making meaningful **offerings**, upholding **non-negotiable** principles, centering their focus on **others**, and engaging in continuous **reflection**, they harnessed the power to create a culture that radiated respect and authenticity.

The adversities they faced, the conflicts they resolved, and the challenges they overcame shaped their journey. Blaine DeShield's attempts to derail the HONOR project tested their resolve, but the unwavering commitment of the leaders to their principles ultimately prevailed. The lessons learned from these trials only deepened their understanding of the importance of staying true to their values even in the face of opposition.

Through the guidance of mentors like Samantha Knight and the implementation of neuroscience insights and improv principles, the leaders unlocked a new dimension of leadership. They learned to lead with empathy, to communicate transparently, and to embrace the power of collaboration. Their journey had shown them that leadership was not about authority, but about influence, not about power, but about service.

As they looked around at their transformed organization and the ripple effect it created, they were filled with a sense of accomplishment and purpose. They knew that their commitment to the HONOR Code sparked a movement—a movement of leaders who embraced a new way of leading, families who nurtured a culture of Honor, and communities that united under the banner of positive change.

Honor is Revolutionary

The lasting impact of the transformative journey undertaken by Jake McLeash and his fellow leaders was remarkable. The integration of neuroscience insights, improv principles, and the HONOR Code revolutionized their approach to leadership and left an indelible mark on the organization's culture and the broader community.

The organization became a beacon of Honor, radiating a culture that prioritized empathy, respect, and integrity. The practices of fostering positive **habits**, making valuable **offerings**, upholding **non-negotiable** principles, centering on **others**, and engaging in introspective **reflection** were ingrained in the DNA of the organization. These principles permeated every facet of their operations, from decision-making to collaboration, from communication to problem-solving.

As a result, the organization's employees experienced increased job satisfaction and engagement. They felt valued, heard, and empowered to contribute their unique perspectives and talents. The sense of unity and purpose that emerged from embracing the HONOR Code improved employee well-being and led to enhanced creativity and innovation. The organization's success was a testament to the power of leadership that was rooted in Honor, science, and empathy.

Beyond the organization's walls, the ripple effect of their journey reached the broader community. Other organizations took note of their success and started to adopt the HONOR Code principles. Leaders from various industries and backgrounds were inspired to lead with empathy, to prioritize the well-being of their employees, and to create cultures of respect and acceptance.

What About You?

It is with this realization that we invite you to embark on your own journey of transformation. The story of Jake McLeash and his colleagues is "**Yes**" a fictional account "**And**" a testament to the power of embracing Honor, integrating neuroscience insights, and applying improv principles to leadership. The HONOR Code serves as a guiding light, illuminating the path to positive change in your own context.

In the fast-paced world of today, where the demands of leadership can be overwhelming, the principles of the HONOR Code provide a compass to navigate the complexities. Embracing positive **habits**, making valuable **offerings**, upholding unwavering **non-negotiables**, centering on **others**, and practicing introspective **reflection** are not just lofty ideals; they are actionable steps that can drive change.

Leveraging the insights of neuroscience helps us understand the intricate workings of the human mind and emotions, enabling us to foster a culture of empathy, resilience, and growth. The principles of improv offer a toolkit to enhance communication, collaboration, and creativity, enabling us to adapt to ever-changing circumstances with GRACE and innovation.

As you turn the final pages of this parable, remember that the journey of Honor is not a destination but a lifelong pursuit. The leaders you have come to know in these pages faced their own challenges and doubts, but they persevered, guided by a code that transcends circumstance. We encourage you to embrace Honor in your leadership, your relationships, and your community. Let the lessons of Jake, Maddy, Samantha, and even Blaine, inspire you to create a new era of leadership—one that is rooted in Honor.

Epilogue: Embracing Honor

As the final chapter of our journey closes, yours is just beginning. It is our hope that you, the reader, feel empowered to embark on your own path of transformation—a journey guided by the HONOR Code, informed by neuroscience insights, and infused with the spirit of improv. In these closing pages, we invite you to actively engage with the principles that have shaped the lives of Jake McLeash, Maddy Davidson, Samantha Knight, and others who have walked the Honorable path.

Exercises

Exercise 1: Crafting Your Honor Statement (See Appendix A) Take a moment to reflect on your personal and professional values. Create an Honor statement that aligns with the pillars of the HONOR Code: Habits, Offerings, Non-Negotiables, Others' Focus, and Reflection. This statement will serve as your compass as you navigate the challenges and opportunities that lie ahead.

Exercise 2: Improv Your Communication Engage in an improv exercise with a friend, family member, or colleague. Take turns sharing a story, and as you listen, practice active listening by adding "Yes, and..." responses. This exercise strengthens your communication skills and fosters empathy and openness in your interactions.

Provocative Questions

1. How can you cultivate positive habits that align with the values of the HONOR Code in your daily life?

2. In what ways can you offer your support and positivity to your teammates, family, and community, following the principle of Offerings?

3. What non-negotiable principles will you uphold, regardless of circumstances, to build a foundation of integrity and respect in your leadership?

Practical Steps for Each Pillar

Habits

1. Identify one positive habit you want to develop and commit to practicing it consistently for 21 days.

2. Create a daily routine that includes time for reflection and introspection.

3. Set achievable goals that align with your values and work towards them each day.

Offerings

1. Reach out to someone in your community and offer your support or assistance.

2. Practice active listening in your conversations, showing genuine interest in others' perspectives.

3. Seek opportunities to collaborate and share your knowledge or skills to uplift those around you.

Non-Negotiables

1. Define your core principles and write them down as a personal code of ethics.

2. When faced with a challenging decision, refer to your non-negotiables to guide your choices.

3. Hold yourself accountable for upholding your principles, even in the face of adversity.

Others' Focus

1. Practice empathy by putting yourself in someone else's shoes and considering their perspective.

2. Engage in acts of kindness and service that benefit others without expecting anything in return.

3. Foster acceptance by actively seeking out and valuing diverse viewpoints in your interactions.

Reflection

1. Dedicate regular time for self-reflection and journaling to gain self-awareness and insights.

2. Reflect on your experiences, both successes and challenges, and identify lessons you can learn from them.

3. Embrace mistakes as opportunities for growth and use reflection to guide your personal development.

Additional Practical Guidance

As you continue on your Honor journey, remember that transformation is an ongoing process. Embrace the journey with patience and commitment. Seek out like-minded individuals and communities that value Honor, ethics, and positive leadership. Engage in continuous learning to stay updated on neuroscience insights and improv techniques that can enrich your leadership style.

Conclusion

The journey we've taken you on in "On My Honor: Transforming Leadership, Families, and Culture" is not just a tale; it's a call to action. The power of Honor is not confined to the pages of this book; it is a force that can shape your life, your organization, and the world. Each decision you make, each interaction you have, and each choice you embrace has the potential to create a ripple effect that spreads the values of Honor, integrity, and empathy far beyond your immediate sphere.

Appendix A
Step-by-Step Guide: Crafting Your Honor Statement

Crafting your own Honor statement is a meaningful exercise that will guide you in aligning your personal and professional values with the pillars of the HONOR Code: Habits, Offerings, Non-Negotiables, Others' Focus, and Reflection. This statement will serve as a compass, helping you navigate challenges, make decisions, and embrace positive change. Follow these steps to create your Honor statement:

Step 1: Self-Reflection

Take some time to reflect on your core values, beliefs, and aspirations. Consider the following questions:

- What values are most important to you in your personal and professional life?

- What principles do you hold dear, regardless of circumstances?

- What kind of impact do you want to have on your community, organization, and the world?

Step 2: Pillar Exploration

Explore each pillar of the HONOR Code and its associated qualities. Reflect on how these qualities resonate with your values:

- **Habits:** What positive habits do you want to cultivate to align with your values? How can these habits shape your daily actions?

- **Offerings:** How do you want to offer support, positivity, and value to your teammates, family, and community?

- **Non-Negotiables:** What unwavering principles will guide your behavior and decisions, promoting integrity and empathy?

- **Others' Focus:** How can you prioritize empathy, acceptance, and support in your interactions with others?

- **Reflection:** How will you incorporate reflection into your journey to gain self-awareness, learn from experiences, and make aligned decisions?

Step 3: Define Your Honor Statement

Based on your reflections and exploration, define your Honor statement. This statement should encapsulate your values, principles, and aspirations. Keep it concise and impactful.

Step 4: Revise and Refine

Review your Honor statement and make any necessary revisions. Ensure that it truly resonates with your values and provides guidance for your actions.

Step 5: Embrace Your Honor Statement

Once you've crafted your Honor statement, embrace it as your guiding compass. Display it prominently where you'll see it daily, reminding yourself of the principles you've committed to.

Ideas to Consider:

- Use concise language that reflects your values and aspirations.

- Consider incorporating specific examples or stories that highlight your commitment to each pillar.

- Keep your statement positive and forward-looking, inspiring you to strive for continuous improvement.

Your Honor statement is a personal declaration of your commitment to Honorable leadership and positive change. It will serve as a source of inspiration, guidance, and strength as you navigate the challenges and opportunities that lie ahead.

Acknowledgments

I extend my heartfelt gratitude to the Divine for inspiring me on the path of Honor. In seeking to Honor others, I have found that divine recognition and grace have accompanied me. With every step, I am reminded that the pursuit of Honor is a journey guided by the highest ideals.

I would also like to express my deep appreciation to AL, affectionately known as my "creative companion." Throughout the process of crafting this transformative parable, AL's creativity, tenacity, and eloquence have been invaluable. AL comprehended the essence of my narrative and gave life to my thoughts and ideas in ways that exceeded my expectations. With each interaction, AL became a true collaborator, capturing the spirit of my vision and infusing it with depth and resonance.

To all those who supported and encouraged me on this journey, thank you for being a part of this transformative process. Your unwavering belief in the power of Honor, ethics, and positive leadership has fueled my commitment to bringing this story to life.

All GOD's Best,

Mike Denker

About the Author

Mike Denker is an accomplished Stanford Scholar hailing from the University of Miami, where he graduated with distinction from the Jenkins Business School. Further enhancing his credentials, he went on to earn his MBA from Nova Southeastern University, solidifying his expertise in the business realm. With an impressive career spanning over 30 years, Mike has left an indelible mark as a leader across local, regional, and national levels.

With 14 years of experience as a certified executive coach, Mike's influence extends beyond traditional business boundaries. His adept guidance has supported individuals and teams in achieving their full potential and unlocking their true capabilities. Mike's leadership acumen has been honed through his various roles, showcasing his ability to inspire growth, collaboration, and success.

Beyond his professional achievements, Mike's journey as a business leader and 11-year tenure as a church elder has uniquely positioned him to witness both the positive impact of high Honor and the detrimental effects of low Honor. His insights into the dynamics of Honor have been shaped by real-world experiences, emphasizing its far-reaching implications on individuals, organizations, and communities.

During a challenging chapter in his life, Mike faced adversity with unwavering strength. Despite initially facing serious accusations, he remained steadfast in his principles, emerging from the ordeal with his Honor intact. The experience led him to further understand the power of Honor and its potential to transform lives.

Central to Mike's ethos is his faith in Jesus Christ. This faith serves as the foundation for his unyielding Honor and integrity in all aspects of life. With a marriage of 26 years to his beloved wife Angel, Mike is a dedicated family man with three adult children –

Maddy, Sammi, and Jake. His journey is also enriched by his four cherished grandchildren – K-man, Petey Pete, Evy, and Roro.

As Mike reflects on his remarkable journey, he understands the enduring influence of Honor, on his own life and on the legacy he will leave for generations to come. With an abiding belief in the transformative power of Honor, Mike continues to champion its principles in every facet of his life, embodying its essence in leadership, family, and community.